Marian McPartland's Jazz World

Music in American Life

*A list of books in the series appears
at the end of this book.*

MARIAN McPARTLAND'S

Jazz World

All in Good Time

Marian McPartland

Foreword by James T. Maher

UNIVERSITY OF ILLINOIS PRESS
URBANA AND CHICAGO

© 1987, 2003 by Marian McPartland

All rights reserved

Manufactured in the United States of America

C 5 4 3 2 1

∞ This book is printed on acid-free paper.

An earlier version of this book was published by Oxford
University Press in 1987 under the title *All in Good Time*.

Library of Congress Cataloging-in-Publication Data

McPartland, Marian.

Marian McPartland's jazz world: All in good time /
Marian McPartland; foreword by James T. Maher.

p.   cm. — (Music in American life)

Updated ed. of: All in good time. 1987.

ISBN 0-252-02801-5 (alk. paper)

1. Jazz—History and criticism.

2. Jazz musicians.

I. Title: All in good time.

II. McPartland, Marian. All in good time.

III. Title. IV. Series.

ML3507.M38   2003

781.65—dc21   2002007126

Remembering Jamie

Contents

Foreword

JAMES T. MAHER

When Margaret Marian Turner was a schoolgirl in Bromley, an old market town in the southeastern reaches of greater London, she was awarded good marks in singing, violin, and piano. The *Kentish Times* reported during 1934 that Miss Turner gave "a lyrical and sincere" interpretation of Mendelssohn's song "The First Violet" at the Bromley Music Festival. However, one of her early teachers testily observed that "this child is unmanageable." To the great comfort of her many partisans amongst jazz enthusiasts the world around, she has remained so.

In the middle 1930s the able young piano student was accepted at The Guildhall School of Music and Drama in London. There she concentrated on composition and harmony, as well as piano, and there she again went her, if not by then unmanageable at least unpredictable, way. She won the composition scholarship of the Worshipful Company of Musicians, wrote and performed a work for piano which she called, with academic propriety, "Valse Gracieuse," and was awarded the Chairman's Pianoforte Prize.

Then suddenly in her third full year she ducked out one spring day to audition for a musical vaudeville act, using the clandestine name "Marian Page" for fear The Guildhall would learn of her aesthetic truancy. She passed the audition and withdrew from The Guildhall, formally, but in haste, leaving behind the piano tutelage, and good opinion, of Orlando Morgan, who despised popular music, calling it "rubbish." She had, capriciously in his view, joined Billy Mayerl and His Claviers, a four-piano ensemble organized and led by a pianist-composer-promoter then well known in England. Her rebellious change of direction brought strong protests from her mother and father. "They were horrified," she has recalled. "But I kept insisting and they finally gave in."

The errant Miss Turner, now one of Mayerl's popular company of music hall pianists, had not forgotten that she had promised Professor Morgan that she would "come back" and get on with her serious study of the piano and its literature. But her promise, like many that one makes in youth to one's elders, was fast slipping out of reach. The ex-student had already crossed one of the most seductive thresholds in a musician's life: she had made her first recordings. Further, she had discovered the joys of being one's own musical self.

To leap briefly into her future, where she was to be very much herself as a pianist, she joined ESNA (the British counterpart of the USO in World War II), switched to the USO after D-Day, entertained troops within the sound of artillery fire at the battlefront in France, toured Allied facilities with a troupe headed by Fred Astaire, performed at Supreme Headquarters Allied Expeditionary Forces (Versailles) for General Eisenhower, and, propitiously, met and married a famous American jazz trumpet player, Jimmy McPartland, whose flamboyant charm was only slightly constrained by the fact that as a soldier-musician he was then performing under orders in the midst of a war.

Enter Marian McPartland, exit Margaret Marian Turner—almost, for she insisted (she is a good insister) on being billed as "Marian Page" in her early jazz career with Jimmy McPartland's various Dixieland/Chicago jazz groups. To clarify the matter of her name: she is still known to her family as Maggie. "'Marian Page?' Oh that was just a name I had made up in London. I can't even remember where it came from. But with Jimmy, I did want to declare my independence as a musician," she has recalled, capping the matter with a witty mot: "If it wasn't 'women's lib' yet [1947], at least it was ad lib."

Leonard Feather, a fellow expatriate and well-known figure in the jazz world as a critic, composer, and record producer, had by then begun tracking Marian's career, carefully and with a certain concern. Writing in *Down Beat* in 1952, he drily, but bluntly, summed up Marian's position in jazz: "She is English, white, and a woman—three hopeless strikes against her." But meanwhile up in Boston, Charles Bourgeois, the *pastor fido* of jazz, was pushing her career along by sending tapes of her work to record companies, with which he had excellent connections. (Bourgeois is well known in the music and news world as the chief of staff of George Wein, producer of the Newport Jazz Festival and its New York successors. For nearly four decades he has quietly shepherded in his own back-channel way a number of careers, all in the pastoral cause of good music.)

A year after Feather's dour summing up, Marian made her professional breakthrough: her trio was scheduled to appear for several weeks at the Hickory House in New York—the engagement turned into ten years of intermittent appearances (1952–62). One night her uncle, Sir Cyril Dyson, the mayor of Windsor (in the shadow of Windsor Castle), came in with his wife. They were in New York for an international conference of mayors. At intermission Marian joined them. Sir Cyril looked around the room with a questioning glance, noting with particular disapproval the big oval bar and the high platform-stage within it.

"My God," she now recalls, mischievously, "I followed his eye and I suddenly realized that when I was up there playing I was almost completely surrounded by hundreds of liquor bottles. My uncle finally looked at me and said, 'Margaret, does your *father* know what you're doing?'"

By the time she settled in at the Hickory House, Marian had arrived in jazz. Duke Ellington (her "main influence") came there to see her and sat in with her trio. Dave Garroway came in, and Garry Moore. Benny Goodman and Artie Shaw both stood at the bar to listen—at different times to be sure. Oscar Peterson came by late in the evening and sat in, as did Steve Allen, Cy Coleman, Kenny Clarke, Oscar Pettiford, and Bucky Pizzarelli.

Three strikes? Leonard Feather (long a principled advocate of women jazz players) had been quite right, yet Marian has prevailed, doing so with style, with graciousness and generosity, with a joyous exuberance that resounds in her playing, and with a personal and musical sensitivity that is abundantly documented in her energetic promotion of other women jazz musicians, in the depth of feeling revealed in her most reflective moments at the piano, in her visits to black classrooms to share the heritage of jazz with the children of its creators (at the same time that she was teaching white school children about this most American of their musical traditions), and, finally, in her lustrous writing about her fellow musicians.

As a child in a proper English home, Marian had been expected to write proper English. There were familial disciplines to that end which she has recalled in tracing her somewhat backstairs career as a writer. "I guess it all started when I was little and we had to write and thank everybody for our birthday and Christmas gifts. My father would stand over me and say, 'You simply must write to Auntie _____ and thank her.' Finally, I would drag myself to the dining room table and sit down. And the letter had to be in good English. It had to be properly written and spelled. And there could be no blots, no scratching out. Make a mistake, start over."

Of such moments are future essayists born.

And, as had generations of parents in setting out their ground rules, Marian's father frequently sought refuge in the time-worn maxim. "He would say things like, 'Fill the unforgiving minute.' That one really got to me. *The unforgiving minute!* To this day every time I hear someone say, 'Oh, I just wanted to kill time,' I wince."

Marian's first venture into writing came as the result of a slightly deflating experience at the Salle Pleyel in Paris. She found herself offstage, a mere spectator, watching a parade of great names in jazz come and go during one of the earliest "jazz festivals."

"It was our first trip back to Europe after the war. Jimmy was on the program—but I wasn't invited to play. So, I was standing in the wings listening—it was a terrific event—and I suddenly thought I'd ask *Down Beat* if they wanted an article on the festival. They wired back 'yes,' and I wrote it as soon as I got back to Chicago."

The article appeared in the issue of July 1, 1949, under the headline "CROWDS JAM PARIS JAZZ FESTIVAL." It was signed "By Marian McPartland," but then four months later *Down Beat* published an article ("BRITISH CATS SOUND THEIR 'A'") signed "By Marian Page," once more her old clandestine self. But whatever her byline, Marian had quite inadvertently begun a time-to-time, second career. A master of self-deprecation, she now says of her Paris fling at reportage, "Maybe I just wanted to be noticed."

Every writer wants to be noticed, of course, but why take on the onerous burden of meeting publishing deadlines in the midst of a very busy jazz career? The reader will find the answer quickly. For even the most casual reading of the occasional pieces gathered herein reveals, strikingly, that the former Miss Turner, laborer in the fruitful vineyards of "Dear Auntie" letters, thoroughly enjoys exploring the exciting and arcane business of music-making—and that she especially delights in talking about her colleagues in the now respectable world of jazz, cunningly drawing out their own surprisingly contemplative observations about their work. (*Respectable?* To be sure. Even The Guildhall now offers courses in jazz. She may yet "come back." And Professor Morgan might be pleased to know that in recent years she has been performing the Grieg piano concerto. One wonders what would he make of her widely admired educational activities and the exemplary quality of her long-running National Public Radio series *Piano Jazz,* winner of the coveted Peabody Award.)

Marian's writing is casual only in its incidental occurrence. Its substance embodies the professional concerns of the author: its style reflects her personality, intense but touched with a lightness of spirit that tends slyly to conceal her serious intention. Further, its variety of subject matter reveals the range and depth of her interest in her fellow musicians and their world. For example, the present pieces discuss (and salute):

—Two outstanding drummers whose names have long been prominent in small-group jazz but both of whom learned much of their cornerstone art in that hurly-burly academy of music, the big band (Joe Morello and Jake Hanna);

—A clarinetist-bandleader who had become a cultural icon after leading millions of Americans into a new realm of music during the depression era, when America sat at home, listening eagerly to the radio with its nightly treasure of free entertainment (Benny Goodman);

—An alto saxophone virtuoso of uncommon lyrical gifts and saber-thrust poignancy whose own fugitive excursions into writing remain masterly examples of drollery overcoming the absurd (Paul Desmond);

—Two thoughtful young bass players then new to the jazz scene and filled with the fervor of fresh musical vision at a time when the jazz world was fragmented by contentious factionalism (Eddie Gomez and Ron McClure);

—A composer, songwriter, and author, a rare old-school gentleman of offhand but weathered elegance whose unyielding good taste, keen intelligence, scathing wit, and almost impossible exactions served as the aesthetic conscience of a generation of singers and musicians (Alec Wilder);

—An ardently remembered pianist who carried introspection to new levels of musical art, thus radically extending the creative reach of jazz pianism, the while reminding one of the evanescent innovations of Fauré, Debussy, and Ravel (Bill Evans);

—The last great music venue on Fifty-second Street during its heyday, the marvelous and raffish years when "the Street" was the center of gravity of the jazz world (the Hickory House);

—A unique, racially mixed dance band made up mostly of black schoolgirls who started out (in the tradition of the Fisk Jubilee Singers) on short fund-raising trips in the Deep South and ended up at the Apollo Theatre in Harlem, where they were embraced by one of the most critical audiences in the country (The International Sweethearts of Rhythm);

—A woman pianist admired and earnestly praised by all factions of jazz as one of the finest composers and performers of her era—the brilliant successor of the pioneer women pianists whose unwritten story goes back to turn-of-the-century New Orleans—an artist of great spiritual resources who sought in her influence on younger musicians to bring order to the chaos of modern jazz (Mary Lou Williams);

—A British film actor renowned for his droll, elfin gifts who discussed affectingly with Marian his reverence for the singing of the late Kathleen Ferrier and his almost equally intense attachment to the music of Erroll Garner—and who learned in an extremely busy life to accommodate and give balanced place to an unusual range of musical abilities. He was an organist (a scholarship winner at Oxford), a chamber music pianist, a choral countertenor, and an occasional jazz pianist (Dudley Moore).

—The other of her baker's dozen articles surveys the past and present of women musicians in the jazz world, a personally committed overview which she rounds off with one of her own wickedly on-the-mark observations: "You've come a long way, baby; but you've always been there."

Altogether a remarkable panorama of an insider's world within a world, presented with the aplomb of a Zen archer who has substituted an outgoing love of the amusing and witty for the inwardness of mysticism.

She has to write on the run—in hotel and motel rooms, in airport waiting areas and aboard jet liners, during rehearsal breaks, or in dressing rooms. Yet despite the pressure of a crammed-full schedule, she is a marvelous listener and, quite obviously, a skillful manipulator of what read like conversational exchanges over dinner. She probes artfully to the essence of her subjects' thoughts about their music.

But one must be wary, for this is more than just a case of colleagues talking from a base of common experiences, using a common professional vocabulary, sharing common hopes. More to the point, it is a case of a natural musician-writer organizing the incoherent flow of good talk into a compelling solo. Cant and windy padding have no place here; no vamping in the wings; no blots and scratchings out.

Although her father may not have known what Marian was "doing" at the Hickory House, he would certainly applaud what she has done in this collection of her writings.

Musician, educator, public radio host, writer: she has filled well "the unforgiving minute."

Preface to the Illinois Edition

The pieces in this book, which date from the years 1960 to 1983, were originally written to show my appreciation of some of my favorite musicians. I'm glad to have this opportunity to bring together in one volume my impressions of them—what they were like years ago and how I saw them then. I've added to each piece (except for chapter 3, which is one of two pieces on Joe Morello) a brief update on their current activities, and it gives me a warm feeling to know that most of them are flourishing, although I think with sadness of those who are gone—Mary Lou Williams, Bill Evans, Paul Desmond, Alec Wilder, Benny Goodman, and Dudley Moore. I'm happy to be in touch with those who continue to create and move ahead, however. I'm also grateful for their friendship and rejoice in the knowledge that they are busy celebrating life and music.

It's been a long time since these pieces were written, and much has happened in the lives of people who are still active and busy. In my case, although I have always done concerts and club dates, traveled extensively, and made one or two new records every year, I have, since 1978, been very busy with my radio show, *Marian McPartland's Piano Jazz,* produced by South Carolina Educational Radio Network and aired on National Public Radio. Some of the people in this book have been on my show, and Mary Lou Williams was my first guest in 1979.

Perhaps it might be timely to explain how *Piano Jazz* got started. It was the late 1970s, and I was working at the Carlyle Hotel in New York City with my trio. Alec Wilder came in there a lot. He had been busy for quite some time taping *his* radio show in Columbia, South Carolina, also produced by the South Carolina Educational Radio Network. The show was based on Alec's landmark book *American Popular Song,* and he was taping the show at the home of Dick Phipps in Lake Murray, South Carolina. The guests were singers such as Tony Bennett, Margaret Whiting, Dick Haymes, and others, and the accompaniment was provided by a trio featuring Loonis McGlohon, a friend of Alec's from Charlotte, North Carolina, on piano. The show was a mixture of conversation among Alec, Loonis, and the guest, and, of course, there were several songs, usually some that had been mentioned in Alec's book. It was a great idea for a radio show, and it was very popular among music lovers.

When the show ended, I received a call from Bill Hay, who was at that time Alec's executive producer, asking me if I would like to do a radio show myself with some other musicians and whether I had suggestions for the format of the show. I had already met Dick Phipps during the taping of one of Alec's shows, and it was decided that he would be the producer of my show. He was an extremely good producer and a very enthusiastic person, and he knew a lot about music, both classical and jazz. After several meetings with Bill and Dick, we decided that the best possible type of show for me to do would be with two pianos, so I immediately started thinking of all the people I would love to have on the show, like Billy Taylor, George Shearing, Hazel Scott, and so on. In fact, with so many people to choose from I was like a kid in a candy store. I was always on the telephone, calling somebody to ask him or her to be a guest on the show. It wasn't until years later that I found out that Alec Wilder had actually been the catalyst who had persuaded Bill Hay and Dick Phipps to be interested in me. Alec always denied this, but eventually Bill sent me a copy of a letter Alec had written in which he suggested that a show hosted by me would be a good replacement for his show.

I wasn't totally inexperienced at interviewing people, having had a show on the Pacifica radio station WBAI in New York in which I played records and interviewed such people as Benny Goodman, Mary Lou Williams, Herbie Hancock, and Eddie Condon, among others, so by the time we were getting ready to do this piano show I felt that I could certainly handle interviews with anybody. Dick Phipps suggested the name for the show, *Piano Jazz,* and that's what it's been ever since.

At the time we were trying to get started, the radio network in Columbia did not have much funding for us, so we wound up doing the first few shows in the Baldwin Piano Showroom on Fifty-ninth Street in New York. Jack Roman, the general manager, was a friend of both Dick and myself, and he offered us the use of the showroom in lieu of a studio, which the network couldn't afford at that time. There were about twenty terrific pianos in the showroom, and I would come in and try them all, then pick two that I liked, and somebody would pull them up side by side. The engineer drove up from South Carolina and set up his equipment in a nearby closet. It's amazing how well it worked. The sound was good, and the atmosphere was great. Although we were in this huge place, which looked out onto Seventh Avenue, we weren't really bothered by it. People passed by, but nobody ever stopped to stare, probably because we always situated ourselves far away from the windows. Also, they kept the showroom closed to the public while we were taping.

I started out with high hopes and chose Mary Lou Williams, somebody I greatly admired, for my first guest. I thought it would be a fine thing to start the series with a woman musician, who had long ago transcended the term *woman pianist.* We had been friends for a long time, and I was sure that she would be a wonderful guest. However, I'd forgotten that Mary Lou could be a tough customer! I think she was displeased because I was the host of the show and she wasn't. In fact, she said to Dick Phipps, in a rather tart tone, *"I* should be the one doing this show!" Dick, always the diplomat, said, "But Mary Lou, you are the honored guest. You are the star." Nevertheless, as Mary Lou strode over to the piano, she was not smiling. The idea of the show was to have two pianos, without a rhythm section, but Mary Lou had brought a bassist, Ronnie Boykins, and she insisted on letting him play through most of the solos and duets. Needless to say I was a little nervous, but I managed to carry on. At one point I said to Mary Lou, "That was an interesting chord you played," and I played it back to her. She said in a haughty tone, "I didn't play that chord," which took me aback. As the show went on, however, she seemed to relax and became quite mellow, giggling and laughing a lot as I had heard her do on many occasions. She even sang a song called "Rosa Mae." This was something I had never heard her do before, and I felt that she was starting to enjoy the show. After we were through, Mary Lou, Bill Hay, Dick Phipps, and I went over to the Russian Tea Room and had a celebratory dinner. At that time I never dreamed that *Piano Jazz* would still be on the air more than twenty years later.

Billy Taylor, Barbara Carroll, and Dick Hyman followed in quick succession. Billy Taylor was a great guest; I think during his years with his own show on WLIB he had developed the easygoing, warm personality that he has always projected. As for Barbara, she and I have been friends for years, and we talked about how we were always working so hard that we didn't notice the "consciousness raising" that was going on all around us and that somehow had never affected either of us. I remember telling Barbara at one point that I was quite jealous of her because she was always working at The Embers on the East Side, which was a very plush nightclub, while I was over on the West Side at the Hickory House, where we had to play behind the bar among the bottles on a very high bandstand and there was sawdust on the floor. We had a good laugh about it, and in later years I came to remember the Hickory House era with great fondness. It was a very important part of my life.

Dick Hyman is one of the most technically brilliant pianists around. We had played together for fun at The Cookery when he was working there. There was only one piano, but playing four hands with Dick then was almost as much fun as doing piano duets with him on the show. He has a fantastic memory for tunes and is known for being able to play in the style of other pianists. He's really one of a kind.

Before we had gone much further, we found out that Exxon was going to be a sponsor for *Piano Jazz,* which meant that we could soon move to an actual studio to tape the show. But before we left the Baldwin showroom we produced some quite memorable programs, including one with

John Lewis, the director and composer of the music for the Modern Jazz Quartet; Bobby Short, who had for many years been holding forth at the Carlyle Hotel; and Teddy Wilson, one of the pianists I had listened to in England during his years with Benny Goodman. After I came to the United States, Teddy and I became friends, and in the early 1970s we recorded an album together for my label, Halcyon. I was looking forward to playing with Teddy again and hearing him talk about his life and times. He was not known to be a talkative person, so I was amazed at how deep the conversation went and how much I learned about him that I had never known.

One of my favorite players was Ellis Larkins, who would occasionally come into the Hickory House and sit in. When he first came to play I hadn't realized that his soft, velvety touch was so exceptional. I guess I had always thought I had a rather delicate sound—until I heard Ellis. I remember that when I invited him to be on *Piano Jazz* he insisted that if he was going to be on the show he must be allowed to stop between tunes and have a drink and a cigarette. Knowing Ellis, I thought it would be best to do it his way! He brought his wife, Crystal, to the show with him, and she had a bottle of brandy with her. I remember being concerned that Ellis wouldn't have enough to drink, so I had brought a bottle of my own. Everyone was very circumspect until the end of the show, and then we all had a few drinks—in fact, more than a few!!! I remember once being on a trip to South America with Ellis, Teddy Wilson, and Earl Hines and noticing how very carefully Ellis spaced his drinks. It was as if he had to keep his thermostat at a certain level and never went above or below that. He was always totally cool. One would never think he had ever taken a drink too many!

We had not taped many shows before inviting Bill Evans to be a guest. I remember that on the day he came I was trying to compose a theme song for the show. Dick Phipps had said he wanted to have a short piece to introduce it, "kind of nervous-sounding or like a group of people chatting." Somehow an idea popped into my mind, only a few chords embellished by Brian Torff on bass. It was almost a blues, and it just seemed to fit the idea of the show. I called it "Kaleidoscope." I was a nervous wreck sitting there trying to compose this piece with one of my idols, Bill Evans, waiting to do the show.

When Brian and I finished recording "Kaleidoscope," Bill was all business, went straight to the piano, ran his hands over the keys a few times, and said, "Marian, this piano is great." With a tremendous feeling of excitement I suddenly realized that I was about to play with Bill Evans. During the whole show there was real empathy between us. It was wonderful! I've listened to this show many times since we first recorded it, and every time I hear it I'm amazed and thrilled at how well Bill and I played together. I'm so happy that I had the chance to get an inside glimpse of Bill himself and the feel of his playing that I would never have got from just listening to him. This interview with Bill on *Piano Jazz* has always been very precious to me; the fact that we actually performed together so well is still a source of wonder, and Bill seemed to enjoy it as much as I did. I have never consciously tried to copy Bill's style, but his harmonic concept and brilliant single lines have always had a tremendous influence on me. The legend of Bill Evans keeps growing, remembered in time—with all the mystery and romance, his memory stays bright, and his music continues to fill our hearts and minds.

Time went on, and more guests came and went—Chick Corea, Tommy Flanigan, Joanne Brackeen, Dave McKenna. I had spent a lot of time trying to play some of Chick's tunes, like "Matrix," but he came to the studio whistling "I Remember You," and it turned out that he was planning to play only standard tunes. Halfway through the show he surprised me by saying he was going to do a musical portrait of me. I hadn't the faintest idea what he was going to do, and I remember saying, "Well, whatever you do, don't put my *nose* in it!" The portrait turned out to be a really beautiful improvisation, and even though I had never tried to do this before I decided I should return the compliment by playing a musical portrait of him. My improv turned out very well, and I'm thankful to Chick for giving me this idea, because since that time I've improvised many piano portraits of other guests.

Tommy Flanigan, who passed away on November 16, 2001, was a wonderful pianist but rather reticent, and he took a while to pick some tunes for the program. When we started the show I said to him, "How are things? Are you okay?" and he just nodded! Not really an auspicious start for a radio show, but Tommy appeared on *Piano Jazz* many times after that and became much more loquacious after that first show. He was actually a very witty guy, and I learned a lot from listening to him play. In fact, I learn from all the different players I come in contact with.

Joanne Brackeen has a totally unique style. Her combination of technique and imaginative, sometimes bizarre, chord changes makes her a challenging piano partner, but somehow we've always managed to sound good together in spite of different harmonic ideas. Surprisingly, we've avoided any "train wrecks," and Joanne's sense of fun is such a big part of her personality.

My first *Piano Jazz* date with Dave McKenna—and there have been several—was during his drinking days when he might, at any given moment, become quite rude and overbearing. On this occasion Bobby Short happened to be in the showroom, and before the show Dave asked him to play the bridge to "I Hear a Rhapsody." As soon as Bobby started the tune, Dave pushed him off the bench and said, "I know that!" Then Dave turned to me in an angry tone, "I'm sick of your British shit. What do you know about fish and chips?" And he kept saying it over and over. "Marian, this man is drunk!" Bobby Short whispered to me. "What are you going to do?" I said, "Well, we'll just do the show the best way we can." So we started and somehow finished the show without incident, and it turned out better than I thought it would. Actually, it was a very good show because Dave's playing was not in any way diminished by his drinking. There was very little conversation, however, except at one point when Dave announced that he was going to play a tune by "Cole Port Hole." Since then I have done two more *Piano Jazz* shows with him, both of which turned out really well. Dave has gotten better with age and sobriety!

Quite a few months had gone by since the start of *Piano Jazz,* the

show was getting good reviews, the Exxon Company continued funding it, and there was no talk of its ending. We moved to the Victor Recording Studio and found it a very compatible place to play. We taped
shows with Dorothy Donegan, Sarah Vaughan, and Cecil Taylor, and I
was trying to persuade Dave Brubeck to do the show. For a long time he
would say things like, "I'll *never* do your show." And I would ask, "Why
not?" "Because I'm too nervous." Finally, with the help of Dave's manager, Russell Gloyd, and Dave's wife, Iola, he did agree, but he insisted
that his son Chris, who was a bass player, should come along in case he
felt in need of support. At the beginning of the show Dave and I started
playing and chatting and having a great time; the whole hour went by
without his mentioning that Chris was in the control room. I guess he
must have enjoyed himself after all.

I'll never forget having Eubie Blake on *Piano Jazz*. I had met him and
his wife, Marion, a few years earlier when we played a four-piano date
at Wolf Trap in Virginia with Teddy Wilson and George Shearing. Eubie was one of the greatest people I've ever known. He was probably in
his eighties when I first met him, and I think he was about ninety-five
when he was on *Piano Jazz,* where he still played a mean piano. He was
as sharp as ever, very funny and full of memories and anecdotes about
his life. He played some of the many pieces that had made him famous,
including "Memories of You," and then I played my version of his tune
"I'm Just Wild about Harry." He loved to talk about his wife and how she
would make him go into the basement to practice; if he stopped playing for a minute, she would come to the top of the stairs and scold him,
"Eubie, you've only been down there for ten minutes." Eubie made one
of the funniest remarks I've ever heard after I fell and broke my hip. He
told some friends, "If Marian was a horse, they would have shot her."
Eubie was really impish—he would tell me that I had great legs, but he
would only say it when he knew his wife was listening.

Later on I did a show with Dudley Moore, whom I adored both as an
actor/musician and a human being. He was on the show twice, and both
times he was a real joy to play with. We also had the members of my

Hickory House trio, Joe Morello and Bill Crow, who traded stories about our good times and played some of our old tunes. By the way, Bill has written two very fine books, *Jazz Anecdotes* and *From Birdland to Broadway*, in which he managed to appropriate some of my best Hickory House anecdotes for himself.

It's hard to believe that I have been a radio person for more than twenty-four years with *Piano Jazz!* It has been a wonderful learning experience for me to play with such artists as Ray Charles, Oscar Peterson, Mercer Ellington—the list is endless. I feel fortunate to be able to invite musicians of great stature on the show as well as up-and-coming musicians and singers. There are also older musicians who are admired and respected but who may not have had a great deal of publicity in their careers, and it's very satisfying to bring some of them into the limelight and find out what interesting lives they have led. For instance, I knew a pianist named Charles "Red" Richards when he was working with my husband, Jimmy, who always called him "Rederine." Red had played with everybody and traveled all over the world with different groups. He was someone I always thought of as the epitome of a true jazz musician, giving his whole life to music, always working, always in demand, yet somehow his name never became a household word. He was still playing solo piano in a club on Long Island up to the time of his death, which came very suddenly in 1999. Red led a remarkable life and was able to talk about a great deal of it on *Piano Jazz*. To me that is real jazz history.

There are others whom I remember just as fondly. One of these pianists was Dick Wellstood, who was truly unique in his way of playing. He had been a lawyer and had a brilliant mind and great sense of humor. Both of these attributes carried over into his piano playing when he finally gave up the law and became a full-time jazz player. His forte was "stride," and it was amusing to hear him take a very modern composition like John Coltrane's "Giant Steps" and play it as a stride piece. He had a tremendous left hand, but his right hand seemed to work independently of the stride style because he often got into far-out and technically difficult improvisations. Dick played with such strength that I would swear the piano actually moved an inch or two when he got deep into a tune! Playing duets with him was an exciting experience.

One of the highlights of my piano series was the day I had my husband, Jimmy, with his whole five-piece group on the show (drums, bass, clarinet, trombone, and Jimmy on cornet), which was the instrumentation he preferred so as to enjoy the interplay with the other horns. Jimmy had always been a wonderful storyteller and raconteur, and he had a great way of putting stories across. Not only that, he had a deep, resonant voice and always sounded very cheerful and upbeat. The music, of course, took care of itself. This was a hand-picked group, and they all enjoyed working with Jimmy. As a matter of fact, going back a few years and remembering the many different players who had been in the band, I don't remember anyone not enjoying himself. Jimmy's lively personality was one of the things that made him so engaging—he was always joking and laughing and generally having a good time. Years ago, when we first started playing together in Eupen, Belgium, during World War II, he was at the top of his form, and I learned a great deal from him about how to play some of the traditional tunes that were a big part of his repertoire. Jimmy disliked the word *Dixieland,* and I can well understand it because there was so much more to his music! He could play beautiful ballads, and when he used the Harmon mute it created a very subtle sound, almost exactly like Miles Davis's. Actually, he and Miles were very friendly. Occasionally, when I was on the road and would see Miles at a concert, he would always ask, "How's your old man?" in that gravelly voice of his.

Jimmy was well liked by everybody, and, of course, I miss him terribly. He died in 1991, but his spirit and philosophy of life are very much a part of me. There were times when I would tell him I was depressed for some reason or other and he would always say, "How can you be depressed? Count your blessings." Amazingly enough, that really does work. One of Jimmy's favorite sayings was, "Do it gracefully." He meant anything from saying good-by at a party to dealing with any situation that called for tactful behavior. I have always been too impatient, so this is something that I try to remember. Jimmy did cute little things like saving the wishbone from a chicken so that we could pull it together and make a wish. I always felt that he was wishing something good for me, little childlike things that made him laugh. I'm left with such good memories of Jimmy, and I find myself wishing I had treated him better and not been so controlling. He went along with everything I wanted to do, and he accepted things far more easily than I did. I always wanted to have things my way.

Years ago when I was on the road, Jimmy was playing an important part in the lives of two young musicians, Scott Black, a trumpet player, and Chuck Slate, who played trombone. They were great fans, and they obviously learned a great deal from him; I know he enjoyed the experience of being a musician/father figure to them. It's apparent that his advice and counsel meant a lot to them, as one can tell from the letters they wrote to him. They have told me that his influence changed their musical lives and helped them to grow musically. Few people are aware of Jimmy's influence on so many young musicians.

So much of what Jimmy talked about over the years was very positive, and his advice has stood me in good stead. "Be yourself," he always told me. "People need to be encouraged, not criticized," was another example of his doctrine. If anything, he was too tolerant of people and the happenings around him. He was not only a fine musician but also a very charitable, sensitive person who would empathize with anyone having a problem in his or her life and try to help them.

Jimmy was also a sports enthusiast whose golf game was in the low eighties. He was an amateur boxer, a strong swimmer, a deep-sea fisherman, and an expert at fly casting. Many a time when we were out in a boat on Pike Lake in Wisconsin, at his friend Squirrel Ashcraft's summer cottage, he would say, "Watch me hit that lily pad." And, just like a kid, he would laugh as he hit the lily pad dead-on. Jimmy had a happy disposition, but deep down there seemed to be this hurt that he had buried years before while he was temporarily in an orphanage, and it seemed to keep him from expressing any anger or frustration. He told me, "I wasn't ever going to let anyone get to me again."

Jimmy loved to take pictures of our cats. He had a Polaroid camera and kept posing one of the cats, Tippy, with his cornet, on the bed or else outside on the porch, where he had trained a squirrel to take peanuts out of his hand. He would stand on the porch and whistle, trying to imitate a blue jay, and he'd be delighted when one would alight on the grass and take the crumbs he had thrown down. These were simple pleasures, but ones that really made him happy.

Thinking about Jimmy and his music always brings a flood of memories—being with him changed my life in ways I never would have thought of. I don't think I would be playing today if it were not for his encouragement and support. In fact, one of his credos was that people should always be encouraged and made to feel good about themselves. Things I never would have imagined have happened, and I discovered that dreams can become a reality. Anything can happen if you work, plan, and keep dreaming. Jimmy did this for me.

Music, friends, and a love of life were always the keys to his many-faceted journey through life, and these continue to give me solace and inspiration. Now Jimmy is gone, but memories of him and his music still sound in my heart and mind. He died as he lived—gracefully.

❖

My thanks to editor Judy McCulloh for her encouragement and belief in me and to my dear friend Joellyn Ausanka, who has given me so much of her time, expertise, and moral support in putting this book together.

And a special thank-you to Nancy Christiansen for her help in researching and preparing the new material for these pieces.

Marian McPartland's Jazz World

You've Come a Long Way, Baby

One of my first reviews as a new jazz pianist opening at the Hickory House in 1952 was by Leonard Feather in *Down Beat*. "Marian McPartland has three strikes against her; she's English, white, and a woman." Somehow this seemed like an accolade! It made me realize that I was doing something unusual and special. But more than twenty years later, thanks to what has been happening to women in jazz, I look at my role much differently. I don't feel I have any strikes against me—in fact, life for me is really a ball!

Of course, the joy and feeling of freedom in playing jazz might never have materialized were it not for the many accomplishments of women in the jazz field who inspired me: Mary Lou Williams, Hazel Scott, Lil Hardin Armstrong, and Cleo Brown, to name a few. These were my heroines—I heard them on records long before I ever dreamed of coming to the United States. Lil Hardin with Louis Armstrong's Hot Five! What fabulous music, and what a dynamic force this woman was all her

Mary Osborne, Marian McPartland, and Mary Lou Williams at the first Women's Jazz Festival, Kansas City, 1980. (Photo by Chuck Anderson)

life to Louis and to other people she worked with, and taught. From Hazel Scott I got my first introduction to an exciting way of swinging the classics by listening to her jazz arrangements of Chopin waltzes. I heard Mary Lou Williams with the Andy Kirk Band, and then with various small groups of her own. She had a strong percussive touch, and whatever she played swung as she produced exciting rhythmic figures and patterns. And as for the somewhat lesser-known Cleo Brown, who, Dave Brubeck once told me, was one of his biggest influences, she impressed me with her powerful, rumbling, swinging attack, colored by full, dark chords.

There were also one or two English women players who were outstanding—Rae Da Costa, a brilliant technician, and Winifred Atwill, who played ragtime. My father liked Winifred's playing a lot, and he'd say, "Why don't you get a style like Winifred Atwill? I can understand the melody when SHE plays." This made me furious.

My very first and main influence was not a woman, but a man—a very great man named Duke Ellington. I'll always be grateful to a boyfriend who brought Duke's and other jazz recordings over to our house and made me really listen; he made me aware of the Ellington band's unique orchestral sounds—the quality and tone color of each soloist—Duke as a pianist—his way of voicing chords—the strong, exciting rhythms of the band. I absorbed it all—and from then on I was hooked!

I had played piano by ear from the age of three. Oddly enough, Mary Lou Williams and I had the same sort of beginning—listening to our mothers play and then trying to emulate them; but what each of them played was a world apart. My mother played Chopin on the piano; Mary's mother played spirituals and hymns on the organ. From an early age Mary was surrounded by jazz musicians, and she grew up in this atmosphere, whereas I went from Chopin to nursery rhymes in kindergarten, to the songs we learned in high school and popular music of the day (Bing Crosby singing "Please") plus everything else on the BBC. When I was seventeen years old, I was accepted at The Guildhall School of Music, where, in addition to piano, I studied composition, harmony, singing, and even the violin. But all the time I kept dreaming about being a jazz player instead of a concert artist.

In between lessons at The Guildhall, I sneaked off and auditioned for one of the "popular" pianists of the day, Billy Mayerl. He immediately offered me a job playing in a four-piano *act* that he was putting together. When I told my parents I wanted to leave The Guildhall and go on the road playing in vaudeville theaters with Mayerl, they were horrified. But I kept insisting, and they finally gave in. Even though the music we played was not really jazz, it was thrilling to be out on my own, a performer!

When the four-piano group finally broke up, I drifted through a variety of jobs, none of them jazz-oriented. I accompanied singers and acts, played in vaudeville and solo piano dates on the BBC, and, finally, in World War II, I joined the English equivalent of USO Camp Shows—ENSA. Eventually, I switched from ENSA to USO and went to France in

1944 with the first show to be sent there after the invasion, and sat in with the GI jazz musicians. In St. Vith, Belgium, there was a big army band stationed nearby, and musicians were talking about Jimmy McPartland, who, they said, was coming to join the Special Service Company in the area in which USO personnel were billeted. I had listened to Bud Freeman, Muggsy Spanier, Sidney Bechet, and Bix Beiderbecke in England on records, but somehow I had missed hearing and knowing about Jimmy McPartland. Then suddenly one day there he was, a good-looking, smiling man in his thirties, just released from combat on the front lines and anxious to play. It's ancient history now, but when he first saw me at the jam session with the GI musicians and found out I wanted to play, too, his first thought (as he tells it) was "Oh, God, a *woman* piano player! And she's going to sit in—I know she's going to be awful." It so happens he was right! In those days I hadn't learned how to back up a jazz soloist. I didn't really keep steady time, or listen enough to the other players. I was so eager to prove myself that I just went barging in with lots of enthusiasm and not too much expertise.

At any rate, Jimmy liked my harmonic ideas (my saving grace), because the army put us together as part of a small group that went out every day at the crack of dawn to play for GIs on the front lines. At last I was starting to get the musical knowledge and experience I so badly needed, learning more tunes, how to play more simply behind solos, and how to keep better time myself. Suddenly jazz records sounded more meaningful. I was able to *hear* more, and to get some ideas from what I heard and put them into my own playing. Jimmy and I got married in Aachen, Germany, on February 4, 1946, and a couple of months later we left for the U.S. to visit Jimmy's family in Chicago.

I listened avidly to all the local musicians and to groups coming in from out of town. George Shearing and his quintet with Margie Hyams on vibraphone came through, and of course I went to see them. This was the first woman vibes player I had ever heard, and she was impressive, showing great technical skill; she played with a beautiful swinging feeling. Later Jimmy and I worked at The Hi-Note on Clark Street opposite

Jeri Southern, a most sensitive singer and a very tasteful pianist. Jeri had a great influence on me. It was the first time I had heard that particular kind of delicate but strong playing, as she accompanied herself without a rhythm section, using her own lush chords.

We came back to New York in 1949 to live, so I was able to meet, and listen to, many of the women musicians in town. Fifty-second Street was still swinging—Mary Osborne, the guitarist, and her trio were at the Hickory House (which later became my home base for so many years); Dardanelle, vibra harpist, and her group held forth at another club down the street; Barbara Carroll was playing at the Downbeat Club opposite Dizzy Gillespie's big band.

With big ears and eyes we visited every club whenever we could. Jimmy and I went to The Embers, which had become *the* place in town, featuring Joe Bushkin and his group. It was an intimate yet noisy room, and I was eager to play there, so Jimmy talked to Ralph Watkins, the owner, about bringing me in. He agreed. I opened with Eddie Safranski on bass and Don Lamond on drums, my first trio engagement. I was nervous and at the same time thrilled to be playing in a top room in New York with two of the town's best musicians. In addition, the job called for us to accompany Coleman Hawkins and Roy Eldridge! These two musicians were my idols for years, and I never dreamed I would actually be required to play for them. It was almost too much for someone new on the scene, but by this time, from my experience with Jimmy, I knew more about accompanying horn players, and now my apprenticeship in other areas really started—learning how to handle new situations; how to play in different styles; finding out the kind of accompaniment different musicians liked to hear behind them; learning how to relate to an audience and how to treat the sidemen.

In those first months, I was eager to do well, and though I didn't realize it at the time, I was very competitive. I liked it when someone would say, "You play just like a man," and I appreciated compliments from other musicians. I even liked it when someone would say, "You play good for a girl," or "You're the best *woman* player I've ever heard." I was so busy trying to play as well as I could that I didn't think about it too much. But finally I asked someone who said "you play just like a man" what he meant. He stammered a bit and said, "Oh, well, you know, I've never heard a *woman* play so *strong.*" Once a man stood at the bar watching me intently, and when the set was finished he came over and said with a smile, "You know, you *can't* be a respectable woman the way you play piano." For some reason or other, this struck me as a great compliment.

These were typical observations expressing the prevailing point of view at that time, and there were many variations. It was thought that women who played strongly in a direct, forthright way were "playing like men." Women were supposed to be tentative or frilly in their playing, yet I've heard *men* who play delicately, with tenderness and a soft touch, who have never been thought to be unmasculine.

As time went on, it became easy to deal with questions from the audience with humor and frankness. Question: "How do you like working with men?" Answer: "I *love* it!" Question: "Does sex enter into your playing at all?" Answer: "You're darn right—especially if you're going with the drummer!" Question: "Why don't you have any girls in your group?" Answer: "One woman is enough, maybe too much." Question: "How can you tell male musicians how you want them to play?" Answer: "I hardly ever do, they usually tell *me.*"

The guys had their share of it, too. Bill Crow, who later joined my trio on bass, was asked: "How does it feel to work with a woman?" Bill, with a sly grin: "Well, I've always liked the company of ladies." Around the same time, a drummer said to Joe Morello: "Man, are you still working with that chick?" (When Joe left to join Dave Brubeck, that very drummer was the first to apply for his job!)

During our long runs at the Hickory House, we spent most of our breaks at Birdland, which was only half a block away, listening to the great bands—Duke Ellington, Kenton, Basie, Woody Herman; fabulous singers—Ella Fitzgerald, Sarah Vaughan, Dinah Washington, and June Christy; and small groups such as Dizzy Gillespie or Stan Getz. I played many Monday nights (the off-night) there myself; in fact the first time I ever played Birdland was with a group of black musicians (trumpet, sax, bass, drums) I had never met. Before the first set we all congregated on the bandstand, and I suddenly realized they were extremely displeased at having me, a white unknown woman player, there on the bandstand with them. It was an unforgettable experience. The tunes would be discussed among them and the tempo kicked off, but I was ignored! Luckily I knew all the bebop "standards," so I just played along, trying to look and feel unconcerned and to get into the music. But it was hard! I'm not sure to this day whom I played with that evening—how could I be? Nobody even said hello! And their backs were turned to me the whole time.

In these busy years, the 1950s, I began to meet other women musicians who came to New York to make names for themselves. The Hickory House seemed to have been a proving ground for all of us at one time or another. I certainly can't accuse the owner, John Popkin, of being unfair to women. When I was on the road, he hired the young German pianist Jutta Hipp, with a trio. On another occasion when I was at the Composer Room on Fifty-eighth Street, working opposite Mary Lou Williams, he brought in a vibrant, hard-driving Japanese pianist, Toshiko Akiyoshi, fresh from the Berklee College of Music in Boston. Another talented player who acquired a big following at the Hickory House was a young Indiana girl, Pat Moran. It was interesting to hear these women, each with her own trio, and observe their influences, their backgrounds, and their particular styles. Every one was different in her own special way, and each used excellent local musicians (all men!). One point worth noting: There has never been any difference in the union scale whether the musician was male or female! The music business is one in which there has been no discrimination between the sexes in this regard. The amount of one's salary depends on drawing power and "name" value, not one's sex.

In those years, girls were not relegated only to trios. Terry Gibbs's big band featured Terry Pollard on piano and vibes. This girl was simply great—she was pretty, and she had a fast musical mind. On the four-mallet exchanges with Gibbs on the vibes, she was brilliant, playing with taste, humor, and boundless ideas. Later, Alice McLeod replaced her, playing in a strong, straight-ahead, no-nonsense style on both piano and vibes. She had a loose, easy, driving beat. Later she married John Coltrane and, since his death, has made many beautiful, intricate-sounding recordings on the harp with her own group.

Many of these musicians influenced me. And so did the girl singers, who can offer a great source of inspiration to musicians, especially by the way some of them have treated certain songs. For example, I could never enjoy playing "If You Could See Me Now" as much as I do if I hadn't heard Sarah Vaughan's beautiful rendition—one of her first big records. "Here's That Rainy Day" made a lasting impression on me when I heard Peggy Lee's poignant treatment of it at Basin Street East. Years ago I started listening to Ella Fitzgerald, and I was especially fascinated by her singing of Gershwin songs backed by Ellis Larkins. What a way to learn these lovely tunes! And how could one begin to play "Easy Livin'" or "God Bless the Child" without a silent thank-you to Billie Holiday? The list is endless. I was eager to learn "While We're Young" after hearing Mildred Bailey sing it. I followed the intricacies woven into "Sweet Georgia Brown" by Anita O'Day when I accompanied her at The Hi-Note in Chicago. Working with her gave me special insight into her way with many songs, which undoubtedly has influenced my playing of them. For any musician, knowing the *lyrics* to a song is important—how can one put feeling and understanding into a piece without knowing the words? For this alone all of us appreciate and admire the many great song stylists—Bessie Smith, Ivie Anderson, Ethel Waters, Carmen McRae, Lee Wiley, and one very underrated singer whom I've always loved—Helen Merrill. And now fresh new singers are bursting on the scene to inspire us—Roberta Flack, Aretha Franklin, Dee Dee Bridgewater, Jean Carn, Esther Satterfield. And there are more and more young women jazz players on the way up.

The same holds true for female musicians. Many people know of Hazel Scott, Mary Lou Williams, and Barbara Carroll, but they've probably never heard of Norma Carson, one of the finest players I know! Years ago she came and sat in with me at the Hickory House, and I was amazed to hear this slim, pretty woman play trumpet in a style close to that of Miles Davis the way he played in the 1950s.

Guitarist Mary Osborne is another underrated musician. For years she was on the Jack Sterling show on CBS in New York with Tyree Glenn and a small band, and during her long stay there she performed consistently in clubs and on records. Mary and her family are now living in Bakersfield, California, where she continues to keep a group together, playing in local clubs.

Mary and many other women musicians have also turned to teaching, and since I am involved in it myself, I can well understand the pleasure they get from it. Vi Redd, the extremely talented alto sax player and singer, lives in Los Angeles and works with retarded children as well as playing occasional gigs close to home. She was on tour for years, first with Earl Hines and his band, later with Count Basie, but she finally had to quit. "My sons made me get off the road," she says with a rueful laugh. "They said they wanted their mother at home and not flying all over the country. I know you have to travel to really make money, but I felt I should consider the kids, so I quit, and now I love the work I'm doing in the schools."

Melba Liston, the trombonist and arranger, has also begun teaching, and she lives and works in Jamaica. She has been an inspiration to many young players, and to one in particular, Janice Robinson, an up-and-coming trombonist from Pittsburgh. Janice is now twenty, and has embarked on a promising career. Fresh out of the Eastman School of Music in 1972, she has been featured with Clark Terry's Big Band, the Thad Jones and Mel Lewis Orchestra, and has played with my groups on several network TV shows.

And what do all these women have in common? All had a musical education. Each has developed her own style, sense of purpose, inner security, flexibility, organization, and knowledge of her instrument. These are the requirements for any musician, male or female—and always have been.

So, how did the misconception start about women players being vague, weak, indecisive, frilly, when it is so obvious that they are not? Mary Lou Williams, who has had to fight this prejudice since her teens, gave me her insight into it: "'Playing like a man' comes from the days when men were supposed to do all the thinking and decision-making and women stayed at home in the kitchen. This was a time when women weren't supposed to think for themselves."

Mary Lou is one person who has entirely transcended the label of "woman musician." In the environment in which she grew up she was steeped in music from early childhood, playing piano with Andy Kirk and His Clouds of Joy while still in her teens, being around great jazz musicians all her life. Earl Hines, Fats Waller, and James P. Johnson were those who helped to instill in her the tremendous creative drive that flows through all her music. These associations gave her strength, encouraged her, and helped to develop her originality. Mary Lou is respected by everybody because she knows her craft so well and everyone *knows* she knows. And it is the reason why she achieved such a high place in the jazz hierarchy so early in life and has continued as an innovator.

Mary Lou once told me: "I used to listen to a man named Jack Howard. He played as if he wanted to break the piano, he would hammer it so, and I thought this was the way to play until I heard James P. [Johnson] and Fats [Waller]. I've always been around men musicians—that's why I think like a man. But that doesn't mean I'm not feminine."

A long-time admirer of Mary Lou's once said, "She had direct, tough, ideas, a sense of organization, of knowing where she was going. But when she walked down the street, she was no *man!*"

Another thing that Mary Lou told me: "When you're playing for people, just be yourself. You must be dedicated to what you're doing. When I'm playing, a spirit comes, and I close my eyes and I go away somewhere. You can't be worrying about looking good—when you're playing, get into the music."

This conversation with Mary reminded me of myself at the Hickory House. There was a mirror set up on each end of the bandstand, and as I played I could watch myself playing and I sometimes did! I guess I must have looked in the mirror once too often—and I know I *was* "worrying about looking good." One night Joe Morello leaned forward and whispered, "Stop looking in the mirror and PLAY!"

I must admit that not only men have shown prejudices against women jazz players. I know of some women who have, too—me for instance! I remember once I was playing a date with Roy Eldridge, and while we were setting up, in came a girl fender bass player! I had an instant feeling of disappointment (how conditioned I was!), but when she started to play I discovered she could really swing! Later, quite abashed, I told the bassist Carline Ray what I had been thinking. I also said, chauvinistically, that she sounded like a "female Ray Brown." (Today of course I'd say just "Ray Brown.") Carline laughed and thanked me for the compliment, and told me some of the things that had happened to her since she first began playing. "Once I was getting my bass out of the car, and a man standing nearby asked me what I was doing. I told him I was the bassist with the band, and he started to laugh! Later, after he heard me play, he apologized: 'I thought you were kidding,' he said."

Just as I thought there were no accomplished women bassists (after Bonnie Wetzel died, that is), I also took it for granted no women played good drums. And so when I heard Dottie Dodgion in the early 1960s, I was amazed at how solid, how swinging, how tasty this woman's playing was!

Dottie and I have not worked together for quite a while, but every time I hear her I marvel at her excellent time sense (at any tempo), and her swinging, hard-driving beat: Dottie is a direct, outspoken woman, with a deep commitment to playing, and her warmth and humor are very much a part of her style. She believes that life is easier now for women musicians, but she is still the victim of ignorance on the part of the average listener.

A customer at a club asked her, after she played her first set, "Do you do this professionally?" And her husband, Jerry Dodgion, the well-known alto sax player, relates with glee his conversation with a fan. Jerry to fan: "You know my wife is a drummer?" Fan: "Really? Well, this guy I was telling you about, he's a *real* drummer, plays good time, and swings. . . ."

Dottie is forthright in her views on women players. She says: "Playing strong doesn't mean *force,* it means solidness. Years ago women weren't supposed to think, and that's what some people mean when they say 'you play like a man.' But most men aren't thinking that! They may secretly be shocked by it, or in awe of it, or threatened by it. But the secure guys can be amazed by it or interested, but *not daunted.*"

Having been such an unlikely candidate for a jazz career myself and having surmounted so many intangible obstacles, makes me realize that *anything* is possible if one has drive, motivation, and is willing to take trouble—to get involved—to be ready to give unlimited time, to learn by trial and error.

Jazz is American music created by the American Negro, not the Africans (although more and more elements of African music are seeping into it and adding new dimensions to it). And all of us—whether we are black, white, male, female, European, or American—have added *our* particular contributions to the music. Each of us is an individual—unique, different—and thus we draw musical ideas from our own personal environment. The kind of life we have lived comes out in our music. Women can, and do, play with "soul," play "funky," swing, and improvise "free" music—why not? We are all members of the same race—the human race—and we must all dig into our own heritage and bring forth the creative gift that is within each one of us.

This is what makes jazz the beautiful work of art it is—so many cultures are a part of it, so many different musical forms, different points of view have been woven into it, only to be changed around, re-woven, re-threaded; adding new textures, given different directions—always moving on to something new and different—and better.

To the women musicians past and present I'd say, "Yes, you *have* come a long way, baby, but you've really always been there."

1975

POSTSCRIPT

Great changes have taken place since 1975 when this article was written. There are so many more women working, not only as musicians but also as television and radio producers, camera people, writers, presidents of corporations, and senators and congresswomen. But particularly in the field of music, women are dominating more and more as conductors, recording engineers, and instrumentalists (singers have always been there), and the attitude of male musicians seems to have changed completely. Women are so much more a part of the music scene now that it seems natural for them to be there, and I believe they are respected and admired even more than they were years ago.

On my NPR show *Piano Jazz* I have been able to explore the lives of many of the women musicians performing today. Some are pianists, some are saxophone players, some are singers who also play piano, guitar, or some other instrument that used to be considered unfeminine, like trumpet or drums. Renee Rosnes, originally from Canada, has become one of the most popular pianists on the scene. I heard her with J. J. Johnson and his group, and she really captivated the audience, receiving more acclaim than any of the other musicians. I noticed how J. J. stood back, a smile on his face, and watched her take her solo. He was obviously delighted to have her in the band.

When you think of a jazz violinist, perhaps the greatest is Regina Carter, while Lee Ann Ledgerwood and Geri Allen are two of the finest pianists anywhere to be found; composer and arranger Maria Schneider has her own band playing her compositions; and Jane Ira Bloom, a brilliant young saxophonist and composer, now heads her own group in clubs and festivals all over the country. This is happening more and more as other women decide to get involved as bandleaders.

In the past, women musicians were often pigeonholed—they either played an instrument that was considered acceptable for women such as piano, violin, or harp, or else they were singers. Now, women take up any instrument they choose. For example, Sharon Freeman plays the

French horn. She works with different orchestras and has made a satisfying career for herself as both a leader and sidewoman. Ingrid Jensen is a highly regarded trumpet player who works and records not only with her own group but also with many other musicians, male and female. She travels all over the world, playing at festivals in Europe and Japan as well as in the United States. She has an exquisite tone and plays with great feeling. Ingrid is also no slouch in the technique department, and she swings mightily.

The banjo is a most unusual instrument for a woman to play, but Cynthia Sayer is a brilliant performer who works in Woody Allen's band and is also extremely busy with her own gigs in various parts of the country. She plays at festivals and clubs when she is not busy with Woody, and she is also a delightful singer. Cynthia is unusual in that she performs some early standards and tunes played by her idol, Eddie Peabody. She has an amazingly wide repertoire of songs and draws a large audience of people addicted to banjo playing. I can't think of another woman who performs in this style with such elegance and verve.

I guess drums would be one of the last instruments that one would expect a woman to play. However, women drummers have been on the scene for many years. I heard Pauline Braddy more than twenty years ago at the Women's Jazz Festival in Kansas City. She had spent several years with the International Sweethearts of Rhythm and was noted for her hard-driving, swinging style. Many members of the Sweethearts (long disbanded) were invited guests at the festival and so were other women musicians and their groups. At one point, Ann Patterson and her band were playing. Pauline got so excited that she jumped up on the stage uninvited and played several numbers with them. It was a real happening, and everyone there could see what a fine drummer Pauline was. In fact, she may have inspired other women to take up the drums, because there certainly has been a proliferation of women drummers in the past few years. I first met Terri Lynne Carrington years ago when she was only eleven. Her father brought her to a jazz club where Jimmy and I were playing, and she sat in and amazed us all with her dexterity and ability to swing at such an early age. A few years later she was leading the band for Arsenio Hall's television show and now is considered one of the finest drummers extant. Cindy Blackman is another brilliant young drummer; she has her own group and several CDs to her credit. Sylvia Cuenca has performed consistently with Clark Terry, and this association has brought her to the forefront of drummers on today's jazz scene.

One of the strongest and most prolific drummers on the scene is Sherry Maracle, the leader of Diva, the powerful and exciting women's band (subtitled, facetiously, "No Man's Band"). Diva has been in existence for several years, and Sherry has led the band from strength to strength, building the careers of other women along the way. Nikki Parrott is the exceptionally talented bassist. Jill McCarron, the pianist, has left to form her own group, so it seems that the band has become a springboard for the careers of many other women players. Sherry Maracle, however, continues to be the heart and soul of the band, which plays to standing-room-only at every venue.

A more recent addition to the musical scene is Dena De Rose, an extremely promising young singer and pianist who has recorded three CDs and is becoming involved with jazz concerts and festivals. I consider pianist and composer Roberta Piket to be my protégée. I first heard her a few years ago at the Thelonious Monk Piano Competition in Washington, D.C., where she performed an exciting and complex original composition. Since that time I have kept in close touch with Roberta and have presented her in a concert at Kilbourn Hall at the Eastman School in Rochester, New York. Roberta is continuing to move ahead and is branching out with various groups that use different combinations of musicians. She is developing a strong and individual style, and I predict a bright future for her.

I have been asked why there are not more women working as "sidewomen," and I realized that people are not aware of the many who are accompanists in groups led by other musicians. I've already mentioned Renee Rosnes, but I should include pianist Francesca Tanksley, who for several years has been the mainstay of the Billy Harper Quintet. Virginia Mayhew and Carol Sudhalter, two fine saxophone players, also come to mind. Marlene Rosenberg, one of the leading bassists in Chicago, works with a variety of musicians, and there are many others all across the country performing as sidewomen and finding the freedom of expression that might not have been open to them years ago.

❖

I was very disappointed to see that so little was included about women musicians in Ken Burns's *Jazz*. Even Mary Lou Williams was barely mentioned, and there was not a word about pianist Lil Hardin Armstrong, who did so much to smooth the rough edges of the raw young Louis Armstrong and who was such an important part of his early life. She performed in his notable group of the 1920s, the Hot Five, and was pianist in some of his most famous recordings.

I feel that the Burns series didn't do justice to jazz; it was narrow and somewhat limited in scope. So much could have been said to inspire the jazzwomen of today who are appearing on the scene, and Burns could have made mention of those who have always been there, some of whom are at the core of jazz, such as Marge Singleton (wife of Zutty), a pianist who played on the riverboats during the earliest days of jazz. Even earlier, drummer Alice Calloway performed with the Seven Musical Spillers and later formed a trio with saxophonist George James and trumpeter Dolly Jones, a player well known for her brilliant tone and execution. There were many ragtime bands in the 1900s that were organized and led by women. Perhaps one of the most notable was that headed by Adaline Shepard, which was called Pickles and Peppers. Pianist May Auferheide led her own musicians, and they played in New Orleans in 1912. "Daisy Rag" and a later composition, "Thriller Rag," were played from memory thirty-odd years later by the great New Orleans trumpeter Bunk Johnson. There were many women's groups and big bands of that era, but, sadly, most of them have been forgotten. Among them, Dolly Jones was the only one who actually recorded. However, some sheet music of their compositions is still to be found.

There were many other female bandleaders during that period, one of whom, Lovie Austin, became a friend and confidant of Lil Hardin Armstrong's. Lovie became a first-rate conductor who could actually write music while conducting. In the early 1950s Lil Armstrong and Lovie Austin, who had not seen each other for several years, were booked together for an engagement. Lil sat down at the piano and said to Lovie, "Well, what shall we do?" Lovie replied without a moment's hesitation, "We'll do it the way we always do."

There are many different cultures in jazz, but the Burns series, for whatever reason, omitted Europeans and almost all women. I've lived through so many eras of jazz myself that I find it disappointing to see so many groups of people excluded. To me, the Burns series didn't bring out the richness of jazz, its global impact, and its ability to cross barriers of gender, age, and race. Rather, it described a period in American history, using jazz as a background instead of putting it in the forefront. Perhaps another producer will come along in the near future who will be more interested in the contributions women have made in the past and who will take note of the talented young women who are bursting on the scene today.

One of the questions I am often asked by women players is, "Who were your influences?" I have had many, some of whom were women. While still living in England I listened to Cleo Brown, who was fascinating to me because of her heavy, rolling bass lines, which contrasted greatly with her highly stylized and sophisticated singing. No matter what she did, she always swung hard. There was Hazel Scott, who made a point of turning Chopin waltzes into really swinging jazz pieces. I also listened to Ivy Benson, who had an extremely popular all-women jazz band in London. I actually auditioned for the band, but I didn't make it! Now I'm really glad that I didn't, but I've always admired Ivy. She kept the band going for many years and always played in top clubs all over England. She invariably had a hard-driving, enthusiastic group of players.

Most of the women I've talked to about their influences have mentioned listening to everyone from Fats Waller to Herbie Hancock, but I think a person's influences have to change with the times. One has to be open to new people and new ideas else it would be impossible to change and grow, and that is the aim of most musicians, male and female.

Years ago people were *surprised* to see a woman musician in a band—surprised and often prejudiced against them. I remember once someone in my audience saying, "I hate to see a woman playing a trumpet, it's so unfeminine." The person who made this statement was a woman! There are no longer any surprises, but prejudice and bias still exist. It's amazing that in this day and age an interviewer will still ask, "How does it feel to be a woman in a man's world?" Unfortunately, these views still abound, but I don't think any of us are offended by them the way we might have been years ago. I usually just laugh. It just seems as if the interviewer has not caught up to the present.

I think the many changes in our society have made it much easier for women to be jazz musicians. Doors have opened everywhere, and there are so many more activities for women to involve themselves in. And involve themselves they will!!! The future looks bright for women in every aspect of jazz and every field of endeavor. We women have staying power, and those of us who were there early in the game can cheer our sisters on as they rise to new heights.

2

Halcyon Days: Remembering the Hickory House

The Hickory House was jammed. Every table was taken, and people were sitting on high stools around the oval bar, drinking and chatting animatedly. Inside the bar, the bartenders scurried back and forth along their narrow pathway, filling glasses and joking with the customers. There was Marty, dark-haired and suave, with a dry wit; and the Dodger, a gray-haired, wiry man who liked to vault over the bar and disappear rapidly into the kitchen when it was time for him to leave. The third bartender was John, the quietest of the three and the one who seemed to appreciate our music the most. It must be hard to imagine that jazz could fit into this setting, but somehow it did.

The bandstand was an island—almost a fortress. At each end of it were large wooden pillars reaching to the ceiling, and around the bases of these pillars were circular shelves holding row upon row of bottles. In the center was our bandstand, and since it was so small, we had the piano up front facing the door, the bass player to the left, and the drum-

Joe Morello, Marian McPartland, and Bill Crow at the Hickory House, 1955.

mer right behind me. Strategically placed on the pillar in front of me was a long mirror in which I could see myself and the drummer, too. It was like a rearview mirror—you could see what was going on behind you.

This musical setting was not exactly intimate. But the people sitting around the bar were glued to their seats, listening intently, and we played just for them. At times I felt like Miss Seagram of 1952, sitting there among the bottles, trying to make my piano-playing cut through the various sounds—the clink of glasses, stirring of martinis, rattling of spoons, and other noises that were so much a part of this busy room. Undoubtedly we got used to it, because there were times when the noise would seem to recede and fade away, and we would be in a twilight zone where we would just listen to one another playing. Once in a while this really happened. The room actually got quiet!

Everything and everyone connected with the Hickory House unwittingly contributed to my growth as a musician. Nearly ten years is a long time to work in the same club. There were periods of what I called "time off for good behavior" when we would be on the road and other groups replaced us, but the Hickory House was our New York City home.

The room was quite large, with a high ceiling and enormous paintings of boxers, baseball stars, and hunters on horseback lining the mahogany-paneled walls. There was sawdust on the floor, and booths that usually held four people were arranged along the sides of the room. The place had a racetrack atmosphere; it was more of a hearty sportsman-type steak-and-potatoes restaurant than a room that featured jazz. Yet somehow John Popkin, the owner, had achieved the impossible by making a success of both good food and good music—and we managed to establish a solid rapport with our audience. As we played, the waiters dashed about, goaded by Julius, the headwaiter. They were all extremely pleasant, and they gave excellent service. The food was terrific—chicken in the pot, boiled beef with dumplings, and the big attention-getter—STEAKS BROILED OVER HICKORY LOGS. On the left side of the room, close to the kitchen, was a huge, brightly lit showcase displaying all sizes and cuts of meat. The bright lights shining on the meat made our little pink spotlights seem dim by comparison. This rather annoyed me, so I would coax Julius to turn the light off in the meat cabinet while we were playing. "I want the people to be able to see the *other* meat," I would tell him.

The music and the room noise seemed to be intermingled. If I had known how to improvise "free" music then as I do now, I would have created a piece incorporating all the different sounds and making them a part of the composition. It was hard to be subtle with the sounds of press agent Joe Morgen arguing with John Popkin, Julius screaming at the waiters, and Howard Popkin behind the bar, manning the cash register, which was a little too close to the piano for my liking. He always seemed to be totting up bills (especially during a ballad), not realizing how much noise he made doing it. The Hickory House was owned by the Popkins, and the family often showed up en masse. When Mrs. Popkin came in, there would be a lot of loud conversation. Sometimes she would be joined by Howard's wife Arlene, plus John Popkin's brother Murray and his sister and her daughter, Roberta, who sang. Once in a while Roberta would get up and perform one or two tunes with us while the whole family sat at the bar, gazing proudly at her. When she had finished, they would return to the back of the room and resume talking at the tops of their voices.

I think John Popkin was happiest when he was in the club by himself or with his racetrack cronies, discussing the wins or losses of the day. I could always tell when he had had a bad day at the track, because he would holler at us for going into the kitchen to get coffee. "All I do is keep you people in coffee," he would growl. Or else he'd look around the bar and say, "Look at them! Beer drinkers!" Then he'd glare at me as if it were my fault that people were only ordering beer. This was probably one of his ploys to keep me from asking for a raise! The hours were long—six days a week, nine till three. We alternated half-hour sets with pianist Ellie Eden, a talented soloist, and usually we all worked on Christmas and New Year's Eve. Yet nobody seemed to think anything of it at that time. It was just part of the job. We would give each other gifts at Christmas, and Julius would buy us a drink. But more often than not we bought our own or sneaked a few behind the bar when nobody was looking. And if the Dodger was in my corner of the bar, he would help.

When I opened in the Hickory House on February 2, 1952, I was told by my agent, Larry Bennett of Associated Booking Corporation, that with luck I might be booked there for a couple of months. But even though I was shy and nervous on opening, something must have clicked, because before I knew it the two months had gone by and we were still there. Actually, that first stint in the club lasted a full year. When we opened, Max Wayne was on bass and for the first month Mel Zelnick was on drums, to be replaced by Mousie Alexander. Max and Mousie had worked with my former husband, Jimmy McPartland, and me in Chicago, and the chance to play at the Hickory House drew them both to New York.

Max was the first to make the move. He had been with Stan Kenton, and this experience had helped to make him a very strong player. I liked his musical ideas and the fact that he could play well at very fast tempos. He was an easy-going guy with a southern drawl, who was fond of telling people he came from "West By God Virginia," as indeed he did. Mousie joined the trio a few weeks after we opened, and it was like a reunion for the three of us. We really enjoyed playing together, and there was always laughter and joking among the three of us. Mousie was a hard-swinging drummer, one who could always be counted on to keep things moving. Everything he did was skillfully executed and tasteful. Time went by so fast it's hard to believe that our trio worked at the Hickory House for eleven straight months.

During that time we started recording for the Savoy label. My first encounter with the folks at Savoy was brought about by George Wein's indispensable assistant Charlie Bourgeois, who has been doing good deeds for me (and a great many other people) since we met in Boston in 1948. Unbeknownst to me, he sent the tape of a 1950 Boston concert I had played to Herman Lubinsky, the head of Savoy Records. The tape was made at George Wein's jazz club, Storyville, with Don Lamond on drums and Eddie Safranski on bass. Mr. Lubinsky liked the tape and wanted to produce a record from it. Although I had previously recorded four sides for the Federal label, I was naturally eager to have a whole album out, so I let Savoy use the tape even though the piano at Storyville was somewhat out of tune. I had made no royalty agreement with Herman Lubinsky, but this didn't stop me. It was my first record for Savoy, and it was more important to me than any financial arrangement. Needless to say, such naivete is now a thing of the past!

Amazingly, I was one of the few people who dealt directly with Herman Lubinsky, although his producer, Ozzie Cadena, would be in charge when we were recording. I remember vividly going to see Mr. Lubinsky at his cramped, cluttered Savoy Records office in Newark, New Jersey. He was a short, heavyset man with glasses and a big mustache, and he always talked to me in an avuncular way about the records and all the money we were going to make. And we did make quite a few records. I'm not so sure about the money, although Mr. Lubinsky told me he had a yacht. Sometimes we would listen to tapes, and I would tell him which tracks I thought we should use and which ones we should discard. He would nod solemnly in agreement and assure me that my wishes would be carried out. Nevertheless, over the years, almost everything I ever recorded for Savoy, *including* the rejects that I had hoped were consigned to the wastebasket, surfaced on albums in one form or another. And they are still floating around today.

Every so often I hear one of the Savoy tracks on the radio, and this calls forth vivid memories. I can see the inside of the Hickory House as if it were yesterday and visualize the people who came in there in those early years. Benny Goodman stood at the bar once in a while, and Artie Shaw came by a couple of times. Barbara Carroll took time off from her classy gig at The Embers to listen to us, and Cy Coleman stopped in often during his stint at the Mermaid Room just up the street. Oscar Peterson sat in, and so did many other players, all of whom were unknowingly contributing to my musical development. Among them were pianist Bud Powell, who often played at Birdland, drummer Kenny Clarke, bassists Wilbur Ware and Oscar Pettiford, and guitarists Bucky Pizzarelli and Sal Salvador.

Duke Ellington's presence in the room was always felt, even when he was not there in person. The club was his hangout when he was in New York. He and his friends would sit in a booth with Joe Morgen, who was the press agent for the Hickory House and for Duke. When I would come over to the table, Duke would cut bite-sized pieces from his steak, spear one on his fork, and offer it to me. He was always making outrageous remarks, which I didn't know how to deal with. He was continually flirting. I loved it, but I couldn't handle it!

On rare occasions Duke would consent to sit in and play. Once he performed one of his early compositions, "Soda Fountain Rag," and another time he played "Night Creature." I sat at the bar, spellbound. At the instigation of Joe Morgen I learned an Ellington piece called "Clothed Woman." This seemed to surprise and please Duke very much. During our years at the Hickory House radio "remotes" were very popular in clubs and hotel ballrooms, and NBC did a half-hour coast-to-coast broadcast from the Hickory House three times a week. This was a marvelous break for us, as it meant that people all over the country heard us and that when we went on the road we already had a big following.

So many memories keep jostling each other for space in my mind. I remember Billy Strayhorn sitting at the bar, always complimentary about the way we played his song "Lush Life." Garry Moore came in often, and as a result we appeared on his NBC-TV *Morning Show* for several weeks. Steve Allen and Jayne Meadows were frequent visitors. Steve occasionally sat in with the trio, and we made many guest appearances on his nighttime television show. I remember, too, fans from various colleges—students from Yale, Princeton, and other schools who would line the bar on weekends. A few of them became our close friends and still are. At the time, their visits to the club weren't always popular with their parents. There was one young man from Yale who would come to the back booth, where we always sat between sets, and would whisper to me, "If my mother comes by, please don't tell her I was here. I'm supposed to be studying for exams up in New Haven." Many of these people still come to see me at the Carlyle Hotel in New York, where I now play, and wherever I go I meet folks who tell me, "I saw you at the Hickory House." I never realized while I was there how much the place and the music meant to so many people. Obviously the Hickory House was a room that will never be forgotten, not only by the college students and out-of-town visitors, but by the many couples who were going together then and subsequently got married. Now, twenty-five years later, they come up to me wherever I'm playing and remind me of those days when they were dating. I'm always glad to see them and tell them kiddingly, "All my Hickory House couples have stayed married."

In 1953 Bob Carter replaced Max Wayne, who moved to Las Vegas. I had known Bob for some time, ever since I first heard him in Chicago at the Blue Note with Shelly Manne and Lou Levy. Mousie Alexander left soon after to join the Sauter-Finegan Orchestra, and I then hired Joe

Morello, a drummer who had already impressed me greatly on the many occasions he had sat in with the group. When I first saw him I thought he looked more like a young physicist than a drummer, but when he played everyone was astounded by his tremendous technique and sensitive touch. We could all tell he was a great drummer. Joe was then and still is one of the finest jazz musicians in the world. I think some of the things that Bob and Joe did then were a little ahead of their time. They would play against the beat, setting up two or three different rhythms simultaneously, while I would just float in and around their rhythmic figures. It felt great! I'd start a tune, Bob would follow and work his way into some rhythmic patterns, Joe would come in on brushes, and we'd be off! There were no bass amplifiers in those days, so in the club the bassist had to rely on a microphone placed close to the bass. Bob had a very soft but compelling sound, and his time was perfect. Everything he did would be a stimulus to Joe to weave intricate figures, first with the brushes and then with the sticks. We'd often discuss playing "on the beat," "behind the beat," "laying back," "on top," etc. Joe would say, "That's all bullshit. There's only one way—either you're playing on the beat, or you're not. Laying back means you're dragging. On top means you're rushing." And he would look at me smugly, because that was my main concern at that time—trying to swing and keep a steady beat.

Actually, one of the swingingest pieces we played was "Love You Madly," a tune Duke Ellington had developed from his famous catchphrase. We made a simple arrangement of it in which Vinnie Burke had a solo and Joe Morello took a couple of frisky four-bar breaks. Vinnie, who had joined the trio after Bob Carter left, was a very musical player. His solos were simple, melodic, and tuneful, and he had good intonation. Joe was already developing the complicated rhythmic figures he later featured with the Dave Brubeck group. At this time he played mostly brushes, and he had a delicate touch—but even with sticks he could play lightly. His technique was breathtaking. Once in a while on the fours he'd do something totally off the wall, which would make me lose my place in the tune. He really would work hard to accomplish this. Having made me miss a beat, he would then get a tantalizing little smile on his face. Years later, I was relieved when Dave Brubeck told me he got just as confused with that same four-bar break.

Things like this would make Vinnie angry. He would look at Joe and mutter under his breath, "The Fred Astaire of the drums." Occasionally in the middle of a bass solo, Vinnie would stop playing, glare at somebody in the audience who wasn't paying attention, and shout, "What's the matter? Don't you like music?" Back would come the reply, "Why dontcha smile?"

I could reminisce forever about the Hickory House. With its closing came the end of an era—it was the last of the great jazz clubs on Fifty-second Street. John Popkin is gone, too, and so are those wonderful moments of music and good times. The Hickory House was like home to me, and I'll always remember it with love. There has never been another place like it, and there never will be.

1980

POSTSCRIPT

This article was written as liner notes for a 1979 Savoy recording (*Marian McPartland at the Hickory House*) that included many cuts from earlier albums. (I am happy to say that it has been reissued and is available today.) I had wanted to re-create the atmosphere of that busy, bustling room that was so much a part of the jazz scene in the 1940s and 1950s. The Hickory House played a great part in the lives of the many musicians who worked there, and I am happy to have been one of them. Now that fabulous era is gone and the building along with it, but in my mind's eye I can still visualize the circular bandstand, the busy bartenders scurrying back and forth, and Joe Morello, Bill Crow (who had replaced Vinnie Burke), and myself drinking coffee and chatting with visiting musicians between sets. I'll never forget any part of it—it was a wonderful time, and I'm sad that it had to end.

Even though the Hickory House is long gone, there are still many people in my audiences at concerts today who remember it and who will tell me proudly that they got engaged at the Hickory House. In fact, many people from those days are still close friends of mine, so it seems that in a way the memory of the Hickory House has not really faded. Bill Crow and Joe Morello are still very much a part of my life inasmuch as we have played some gigs together through the years, they have been on my radio show *Piano Jazz,* and they were a big part of my eightieth birthday celebration concert at Town Hall in New York City.

That reunion gave me the idea to make a new CD featuring some of those same Hickory House tunes that we had played forty-five years earlier. In the beginning it seemed like a joke, but when I mentioned it to the people at Concord Records they loved the idea, so we booked a date at Birdland and recorded live for two nights in September 1998. It turned out to be a very successful date, and even Joe, the perfectionist that he is, seemed to be pleased with the overall result. We called the CD *Reprise,* and it is in great demand, especially because of Joe, who takes some brilliant solos, including one "free" piece that the two of us played together.

For many reasons it seems that the Hickory House will always be in our memories. Many of my college fans of those years now come to my concerts with their children and even grandchildren. It's really heart-warming to have been a part of such an important time in jazz history that has meant so much to so many people, reminding us of happy times and music well played.

The Fabulous
Joe Morello

3

The French they are a funny race. And drummer Joe Morello, who is of French extraction, does nothing to confound the maxim. His Gallic characteristics, combined with his quiet New England upbringing, seem to be at the root of his personality—high-spirited, full of fun, yet serious and sensitive to a marked degree.

In Joe Morello there is a dreamer who is nonetheless a down-to-earth realist; someone who is reserved yet outspoken; shy much of the time, yet frequently completely uninhibited.

These are not just characteristics that set Joe apart as a man. They also help to set him apart as a jazz musician—one who leaves critics and fellow workers alike raving about his fantastic technical ability, his taste, his touch, and his ideas.

Joe was born, brought up, and went to school in Springfield, Massachusetts. His father, now retired, was a well-to-do painting contractor

Joe Morello. (Photo by
Joseph L. Johnson)

who had come to the United States from the south of France. Joe's mother, who died when he was seventeen, was French-Canadian.

A gentle, music-loving woman who taught him as a small boy the rudiments of piano playing, she encouraged and fostered his obvious love for music. She saw that many of the pleasures others find in life would be impossible for Joe: his extremely poor vision prevented him from participating in most of the games and sports other children enjoyed. Music, she seemed to feel, was the best compensation—and perhaps much more than mere compensation.

When Joe was seven, his parents bought him a violin, and he began to show a precocious talent for and interest in music. Moody and withdrawn, he disliked school and made few friends. One friendship he did form, however, was with a neighbor, Lucien Montmany, a man who, crippled and confined to his home much of the time, took a great interest in the boy. He would play piano for him by the hour, and encouraged him to pursue music.

"Bless his soul, he was such a wonderful guy," Morello said. "And he helped me so much. He gave me confidence in myself, and after I had started studying drums, he used to say to me, 'Joe, you've got to practice all you can now, because you won't have the time later on.'

"And you know, he was right."

But Joe did not become interested in the drums until he was about fifteen. Until that time, he remained preoccupied with piano and violin—which explains in part the musicality of his work and his extreme sensitivity to other instruments.

He had made a few cautious forays into the rhythmic field. But these efforts were largely confined to performing with a couple of spoons on the edge of the kitchen table, as accompaniment to phonograph records. It irritated his parents and his sister, Claire, considerably.

But at last, with money earned from an after-school job in a Springfield paint shop, he bought himself a snare drum, sticks, and brushes and later—with money gained from the diligent selling of Christmas cards, among other things—the rest of the set. He found a teacher, Joe Sefcik, and began sitting in around town.

It was about this time that Morello formed a close friendship with another man who was to emerge as an important name in jazz: guitarist Sal Salvador.

"It was sometime in 1946 that I met Joe," Salvador recalled recently. "I was playing one of my first jobs when he came into the club with his father. He must have been about seventeen. I remember his father tried to get him to sit in, but he hung back.

"But finally he did agree to sit in, and he had very good chops even then. It was Joe Raiche's band. He was pretty well the king around Springfield, but we had heard talk about Joe Morello. And so he and Joe Raiche played some fours, and everybody thought he was great. I really dug what he did with the fours, especially since he was only playing on the tom-

tom, and I asked him about working a job with me. After that we kept calling each other for jobs which we never seemed to get.

"From then on we were inseparable, we saw each other all day, every day."

Salvador tells several amusing stories that illustrate how much Joe (and several of his friends) wanted to play.

"Teddy Cohen [Teddy Charles], Chuck Andrus, Hal Sera, Phil Woods, and Joe and I would all get together and play as often as we could," he said. "Saturday afternoons we used to go to Phil's house. One day it was so hot that we moved the piano out onto the porch. Joe moved his drums out there, too. The weight was too much. The porch tipped! Everyone panicked.

"But Joe was the first to recover. And he was the first one back indoors, with his drums set up to play.

"We were so anxious to play that we'd set up and start things going just anywhere we could. Once we drove out to a club called the Lighthouse. But it was closed when we got there, so we set up and started playing, right in front of the place.

"Pretty soon the cops came and chased us away. I guess we kids just didn't think about what the grownups had to go through with us in those days."

Morello and Salvador continued working together at an odd assortment of jobs, including a radio broadcast, dances, and square dances. "Anything we could get," Salvador said. Then Morello started going to Boston to study with a noted teacher named George Lawrence Stone.

"I think it was Mr. Stone who finally made him realize that sooner or later he would have a great future in jazz," Salvador said. "And, of course, he gave Joe this great rudimental background. In fact, Joe became New England rudimental champion one time.

"In 1951 he joined Whitey Bernard. Finally, after working on the road with him, he went to New York in 1952 and put in his union card. I had gone there and had been begging him to come for some time. But he would say, 'No, I'm not ready yet. There are too many good drummers there.'

"However, he finally made it, and as you know, the Hickory House was one of the first places that he and I came to, to hear your group."

From here on, Joe Morello's story becomes quite personal to me.

At the time, there was a constant swarm of musicians at the bar of the Hickory House, where I was working. Sal had often told me about this "fabulous" drummer from Springfield. But being so accustomed to hearing the word *fabulous* used to describe talent ranging from mediocre to just plain bad, I was slightly skeptical.

But one night Joe came in with Sal. Mousie Alexander, who was playing drums with me at the time, introduced us. Joe Morello, a quiet, soft-spoken young man about twenty-three, looked less like a drummer than a student of nuclear physics. Yet I was, after hearing so much about him, eager to hear him play.

We got up on the stand, Joe sat down at the drums and deftly adjusted the stool and the cymbals to his liking. And we started to play.

I really don't remember what the tune was, and it isn't too important. Because in a matter of seconds everyone in the room realized that the guy with the diffident air was a phenomenal drummer. *Everyone* listened.

His precise blending of touch, taste, and an almost unbelievable technique were a joy to listen to. His technique was certainly as great (though differently applied) as that of Buddy Rich. And through it all, he played with a loose, easy feeling interspersed with subtle flashes of humor reminiscent of the late Sid Catlett.

That is the way Joe sounded then, and I will never forget it. Everyone knew that here was a discovery.

Word of his amazing ability spread like fire among the musicians, and soon he was inundated with offers of work. It was not long afterwards, following a short period with Stan Kenton's band and some dates with Johnny Smith's group, that Joe became a regular member of my group.

We opened at the Blue Note in Chicago in May 1953 and later returned to the Hickory House.

Every night it was the same thing: the place was crowded with drummers who had come to hear Joe.

He practiced unceasingly between sets, usually on a table top, with a folded napkin to deaden the sound and prevent the customers and the intermission pianist from getting annoyed. Sometimes the owner would walk over and say irascibly, "Stop that banging!"

But usually no one bothered him, and he gave his time generously to the drummers who came to talk with him. Soon he had some of them as pupils.

And wherever we played it was the same. Young drummers appeared as if by magic to listen to Joe and talk to him and to study. They arrived at all hours, in nightclubs, at television studios, in hotels. We called them "the entourage." Several of them now are playing with top groups in various parts of the country.

During this period, Joe, bassist Bill Crow, and I started doing a lot of television and recorded several LPs for Capitol. Nineteen-fifty-five was a good year for us. We received the *Metronome* small group award, and Joe won the *Down Beat* International Critics poll new star award. It was presented to him on the *Steve Allen Show.*

About that time, Joe and Bill were making so many freelance record dates that I told them I thought I should open an office and collect 10 percent!

Some of Joe's best work was done on those sessions. At least, the best I have heard him play. There is a wonderful recording that he and Bill made with Victor Feldman and Hank Jones which, unfortunately, never has been released.

But there are other albums in which you can hear Joe at this period. One was an album done by Grand Award, with a group led by trombonist Bob Alexander. "Chloe" is easily the finest track. There's an interesting vocal and drum exchange with Jackie Cain and Roy Kral in a piece called "Hook, Line and Snare" in an album they did together. And he recorded some sides with my husband Jimmy and myself. This was more on the Dixieland kick, which points up Joe's extreme flexibility.

There are also some wonderful sides Joe made with Gil Melle, Sal Salvador, Sam Most, Lou Stein, John Mehegan, Tal Farlow, Helen Merrill (with Gil Evans's arrangements), and with Jimmy Raney and Phil Woods.

Alas, though for a time he turned down all offers, I was not to keep Joe with my group forever. And when I lost him as my drummer, my one consolation was that he was going to join a musician whom I respected very deeply: Dave Brubeck.

Joe joined the quartet in October 1956. Since then he has gone on growing. Indeed, his playing has altered considerably, partly because of his fanatical desire for improvement and change, partly because the kind of playing Dave requires from a drummer is different from the techniques that Joe used with my group.

With me, Joe had concentrated more on speed, lightness of touch, and beautiful soft brush work. Dave, both a forceful personality and player, requires a background more in keeping with his far-reaching rhythmic expositions and someone who can match him and even surpass him on out-of-time experimentation.

Today, Joe, though a complete individualist, hews closely to Dave's wishes as far as accompaniment is concerned. But he cannot help popping out with little drummistic comments, subtle or explosive, witty or snide—depending on his mood at the moment.

It is Dave's particular pleasure to go as far out as possible in his solos and have the rhythm section carry him along. For this reason, the drummer must have a very highly developed sense of time and concentration to keep the tune moving nicely while these explorations are under way.

Bassist Gene Wright and Joe—"the section" as they refer to each other—do this most ably. Wright's admiration for Joe is unbounded.

"There's never been any tension at all from the day I joined the group," he said. "Joe makes my job very easy. We play together as one, and when a drummer and bass player think together, they can swing together. As a person, he's beautiful, and it comes out in his playing.

"There are no heights he cannot reach if he can always be himself and just play naturally. His potential is far beyond what people think he can do, and he'll achieve it some day."

Like any musician, Joe has detractors, those who can be heard muttering to the effect that he's a great technical drummer but doesn't really lay down a good beat—or, in more popular parlance, "He don't swing, man." But these detractors are remarkably few, and Brubeck is vehement in saying, "They're out of their minds!"

"Joe swings as much as anybody," Dave said, "and he has this tremendous rhythmic understanding. You should have heard him over in India with the drummers there. They just couldn't believe an American drummer could have that kind of mind, to grasp what they were doing. They said it would probably only take him a little while to absorb things it had taken them a lifetime to learn.

"As it is, Joe assimilates things quicker than any jazz musician I know, and he has the biggest ears. He was able to do many of the things the Indian drummers were doing, but they couldn't do what he does because they're just not technically equipped for it.

"How has his playing affected my group?

"I would say we have a better jazz group since Joe joined us. He really *pushes* you into a jazz feeling. And in his solos, when he gets inspired, he does fantastic things. Sometimes he gets so far out it's like someone walking on a high wire. Of course, he doesn't always make it, and then he'll say, 'Oops!' But then he'll come right back and do it next time around. He is a genius on the drums."

Paul Desmond is just as forthright in his comments about Joe. "Joe can do anything anybody else can do, and he has his own individuality, too," Brubeck's altoist said. "Do we usually play well together? Yes, unless we're mad at each other! Naturally there are times, as in any group, when there might be a little difficulty of rapport if we are feeling bad. Playing incessantly, the way we do, night after night, it's almost impossible once in a while not to be bored with each other and with one's self. This is never true of Joe, especially on the fours."

I asked Paul how he felt about the rave notices that Joe has been getting since he joined the group.

"Well, Dave and I have been on the scene for about ten years now," he replied, "and it's only natural that somebody new, especially a drummer as good as Joe, would rate the attention of the critics. He definitely deserves all the praise he is getting. I think he's the world's best drummer, but it's his irrepressible good humor on and off the stand that I dig most of all."

Similar views were shared by a good many other persons, among them Joe's friend and long-time co-worker at the Hickory House, bassist Bill Crow, though he expresses it a little differently.

He always has amazingly precise control of his instrument at any volume, at any tempo, on any surface, live or dead. He's very sensitive to rhythmic and tonal subtleties and has a strong time sense around which he builds a very positive feeling for swing. Extraordinarily aware of the effect of touch on tone quality, he uses his ears and responds with imagination to the music he hears associates play.

With these assets, I nevertheless feel Joe isn't a finished jazz drummer, considering his potential. He can play any other kind of drum to perfection, but I don't think he's saying a quarter of what his talent and craftsmanship would inevitably produce if he were playing regularly with musicians who base their rhythmic conception on the blues tradition.

I know that Joe is attracted to this tradition, uses it as a focal point in his establishment of pulse, and feels happiest when he is playing with musicians who work out of this orientation. But he has never yet found a working situation where anyone else in the band knew more than he did about the subtleties of it . . .

He still has to find an environment that would demand response and growth on a deeper level. He needs to solve the problems presented by soloists like Ben Webster, Sonny Rollins, Harry Edison, or Al Cohn. He has to discover from his own experience how the innovations of Dave Tough, Sid Catlett; Kenny Clarke, or Max Roach can be applied to various musical situations. But primarily, he needs to play with Zoot Sims–type swingers who will reaffirm his feeling for loose, lively time.

Now that Joe's home base is San Francisco, he and his wife Ellie (they were married in 1954 while we were playing at the Hickory House) maintain an apartment in town. They have formed a close friendship with Ken and Joan Williams, owners of a San Francisco drum supply shop where Joe teaches every day he's not on the road and where he practices incessantly. The feeling his pupils have for him is nothing short of hero worship, and his opinions and views are digested word for word.

As Sam Ulano, a noted New York drum teacher, puts it, "One of the great things Joe has done to influence the young drummers is to make them more practice conscious. He has encouraged them to see the challenge in practice and study, and I think it is important, too, that people should know how Joe has completely overcome the handicap of poor vision to the extent that few people are even aware of it. This disability has acted as a greater spur to him, already filled as he is with deep determination to perfect his art, and others with similar problems can take note and gain hope and encouragement from it."

A conversation with Joe, no matter on what subject, invariably comes back to a discussion of music in one form or another. Musicians for whom he has veneration and respect range from veteran drummers Gene Krupa and Jo Jones to pianists Hank Jones, Bill Evans, and John Bunch. Phil Woods is one of his favorite horn players, and he admires Frank Sinatra, Peggy Lee, Anita O'Day, and Helen Merrill. His tastes in music run from plaintive gypsy violin music to the Brandenburg concertos.

Joe confesses to a dream for the future of having his own group. He would like to have his long-time friend, altoist Woods, in it.

> But I'm not really ready for this yet. What I'd like to do right now is to develop greater facility, plus ideas, and improve my mind musically. To have basically good time—that's the first requisite, of course. Taste comes with experience. Then, too, you must have a good solid background to enable you to express yourself properly.
>
> This is one of the things Mr. Stone did for me when I studied with him, and I owe him a great deal. He taught me how to use my hands. My idea of perfection would be good time, plus technique, plus musical ideas. Technique alone is a machine gun! But it sure brings the house down.

Years ago I was impressed by technique more than anything else. I think what made me go in for this so much when I was working with you, Marian, was that I was shocked by the lack of it in the New York drummers. I didn't realize at the time that a lot of them might be thinking more musically and developing along other lines. Now I listen for different things and I try to think of a musical form in my solos—a musical pattern. And when you know you're right, and it feels good to you without sounding mystical or corny, sometimes things just come rolling out—building and building—a sort of expansion and contraction, you know? Now, take Buddy [Rich]. If you want to use the term great, he's great. And Shelly [Manne]—I admire him very much and Louis Bellson, too.

Years ago Joe Raiche and I went to see Louis at Holyoke, and we invited him back to the house. I'd started experimenting with the finger system, but he really had it down, and as we sat at the kitchen table and talked, and he showed me some things. I sometimes think I played better in Springfield than I do now, though I've learned an awful lot from playing with Dave and Paul [Desmond], and Dave's such a good person to work for.

Being with this group is a marvelous experience for me. I'm grateful for the freedom Dave gives me, and he does give me plenty, both in concerts and on the albums. Working with him is interesting because he's very strong in what he believes in. But then so am I, and we both know this. So we respect each other's views, and we compromise—each of us gives a little. And as Dave said to you, we've found a point of mutual respect and understanding. We know we don't agree completely, and yet we can go on working together and enjoying it.

There's so much to be done—if you've got the mind and the imagination. That's what the drummer needs—the *mind!* And talent? You know what that is? It's $97^{1}/_{2}$ percent work and $2^{1}/_{2}$ percent b.s.

I want to be as musical as I can—play the best I can for the group I'm with—and be myself. If I can do that, then I'll be happy.

1960

Joe Morello:
With a Light Touch

Joe Morello is a man of many natures. Restless, quiet, at times effervescent, at others the life of the party or completely aloof. Like the dark side of the moon, there is much about him that is unknown to most persons, perhaps even to himself. Yet he is also naive and funny. One moment, he will exclaim, with a schoolboy grin, "I feel like a sick sailor on the sea of life." Two minutes later, he will mutter moodily, "I should have been a monk." One could use a divining rod, sextant, sundial, geiger counter, and crystal ball to anticipate—and keep track of—the many verities of his nature.

To many young drummers, he is like a savior. Accordionist-organist-singer Joe Mooney calls him the "well-dressed metronome." To his detractors he is merely a gifted drummer, an exceptional technician who can be hostile, even arrogant, at times. He has been called a prima donna whose mood can change from animation to black despair without notice.

But people who know him well know, too, that he is also gentle, idealistic, and sensitive, a searcher for something he cannot name, who daydreams dreams, many of which already have come true.

"Do you know—I'm the only drummer who ever won the poll who doesn't have his own band?"

Morello says that with a big grin. Having made a clean sweep of most jazz popularity polls three years running—including *Down Beat*'s Readers Poll—one would imagine he is delighted with the way things are going, especially since he has the salary and prestige of many a leader with few of the responsibilities. Possibly the highest paid and certainly one of the most respected and admired drummers in the country, he can afford to smile.

"I've been lucky," he says. But anyone who knows Morello knows well that hours of practice, rigid discipline, and a continuing pursuit of perfection have had more to do with his current eminence than simple luck.

Further goals are pictured clearly in his mind's eye: "I can always see that straight line, and then I know I'm right."

Joe has been guided in this intuitive fashion many times, first perhaps when he decided to give up violin in favor of drums, overruling his father's original wish that he should become a painting contractor. Later, he decided to go to New York City ("I told my father I'd give myself six months to make good—if I didn't, I was going to go back to Springfield"). Later still, he joined my trio and while with it from 1953 to 1956 started to build the reputation he now enjoys. With growing confidence, he felt ready, in 1956, to join Dave Brubeck, with whose quartet he has established himself as a percussion virtuoso.

The publicity and acclaim he has received over the last nine years has been of inestimable value to him, for Joe, outstanding as he is, needs a showcase for his talents, and Dave has been more than generous. Dave has shared his spotlight with Joe and given him ample solo space. No leader could have been more considerate.

Though undoubtedly grateful, Joe has made full use of the spotlight, even to the extent of some artless scene-stealing—twirling the sticks, shooting his cuffs during a piano solo, delicate sleight of hand with the brushes, and other diversionary tactics.

However, Joe is probably the one drummer who has made it possible for Dave to do things with the group that he would have had difficulty accomplishing otherwise. Joe's technique, ideas, ability to play multiple rhythms and unusual time signatures, humor, and unflagging zest for playing are a combination of attributes few other drummers have. All these in addition to his ability to subjugate himself, when necessary, to Dave's wishes yet still maintain his own personality.

Joe is fascinating to watch play—he may have several rhythms going at one time, tossing them to and fro with the studied casualness of a juggler. Yet through it all, the inexorable beat of the bass drum (not loud—felt more than heard) holds everything together. He moves gracefully, with a minimum of fuss, but with a sparkling, diamond-sharp attack reminiscent of the late Sid Catlett.

Sometimes a quick, impish grin comes over his face as he plays a humorous interpolation, and then he looks for all the world like a small boy throwing spitballs at his classmates. Though he seems withdrawn—remote at times—his movements are so expressive that when he breaks into a smile and glances around at Gene Wright, the group's bass player, one can sense his pleasure and can be a part of it.

Despite Joe's varying emotions and changing moods, there is one thing about him that never changes, except to grow stronger: his love of playing. This love is reflected in everything he does, his approach to life, to people, to himself.

As long as I have known Joe, he has had fine musical taste, technical control, and a light touch "delicate as a butterfly's wing," to quote Dave Garroway, and though he plays a great deal more forcefully with Brubeck than he did with my trio, still the lightness is there most of the time.

"Underplay if possible," he told me recently. "If you start off at full volume, you have nowhere to go. Be considerate of the other members of the group—drums can be obnoxious or they can be great."

Where Joe is concerned it is invariably the latter. I have never heard him play badly.

Now that he is, in the eyes of many, the No. 1 drummer in the country, he could be the man to change the course of current drumming. In this era, when sheer volume appears to be the criterion for percussion excellence, when the artisan has apparently been replaced by the unschooled, Joe Morello stands out as something of a phenomenon. He is not an innovator, but he draws from the styles of drummers past and present whom he has observed and admired to produce a sound, a touch, a feeling that is essentially his own.

He has been criticized rather than praised by some of his peers, who tend to enjoy a barrage of sound, crudely produced, rather than the finesse, delicacy, and range of dynamics that Joe draws from drums. Nevertheless, it may be that he is, in the words of drum manufacturer Bill Ludwig, "an apostle—someone who can preach the word to all the kids coming up, show them how to play the drums properly, how to play cleanly, to direct their studies and their talents to the most musical approach to the drums possible."

In the last few years, he has had opportunity to talk with novice and would-be drummers and to show them some of his ideas.

They crowd around him after concerts. They dog his footsteps in hotels. They gather in dining rooms and coffee shops. Joe also gets three months a year off from the Brubeck group and travels the country to appear at drum clinics in schools, music stores, and auditoriums for the benefit of the local drummers, students, and teachers.

The clinic idea is not new, but Joe has brought a different dimension to it. From being a comparatively small operation in which possibly a hundred persons would come to see a name drummer play a solo and perhaps give a short talk, clinics are now getting to be big business. When Joe appears at one, the hall is invariably jammed; if the room holds five hundred, another two hundred are turned away. Last year Joe pioneered the clinic idea in several European countries—England, Holland, Germany, and Denmark. More recently he has brought drum clinics to Puerto Rico. This year he will give clinics in new territory—when the Brubeck quartet goes to Australia, New Zealand, and Japan.

Everyone associated with the clinics is happy. "For every one that he does, I could book ten," said Dick Schory of the Ludwig Drum Company, Morello's sponsor. "There has never been a drummer who can draw people like he does, and he can keep them on the edge of their seats for two hours. He's a very good extemporaneous speaker, and he's such a ham that I'm sure he'd rather do this than play the drums. He razzles and dazzles them with his playing, and he has this fantastic sense of humor—it's not dry-as-dust lecturing—he makes it interesting, and he believes in it."

He will relax the crowd at the start of the clinic by kiddingly referring to it as a "hospital for sick drummers—and I'm the sickest of them all." Or "I guess all you people must need help or you wouldn't be here." Last year in London, at the first clinic there, he greeted deafening applause with, "If I'm elected, I promise. . . ." After a particularly sizzling display, which had everybody on his feet applauding, he shook his head morosely and muttered, "I must be getting old."

Joe usually divides the two-hour lecture into several parts—first describing his drum set-up, what size the drums are and why he uses them. Once in a while he will do impressions of well-known drummers with devilish accuracy. Sometimes he plays a short but hilarious solo, doing everything wrong, to expose areas in which a drummer could improve. He answers questions tirelessly and takes great pains to make sure that everyone has understood his meaning, going over a point several times if necessary.

"I'd like to have him do these clinics all the time," Bill Ludwig said. "He's a natural teacher, and he's at his best with kids. Nothing is too much trouble—he loses himself in it. This is the answer to the uneducated drummers of today show them what real study is.

"As far as actual talent is concerned, there hasn't been anyone quite like him—no one who has this devotion to the instrument. And he's such a gentleman.

"He has brought realism to the clinics; he's not just a performer who will pass the two hours giving a technical demonstration. This guy opens his heart and says, 'Here it is, use it, free.' I've seen clinicians who would spend two hours showing off their dexterity, but Joe does things that are useful to the students."

One can only guess at Joe's feelings about this acclaim. It surely has not changed his attitude toward his work. He has never let up. When at home, it's still practice, practice. He seems to derive comfort from this, almost as if the drums were a refuge where he feels secure and can gain reassurance.

The standing ovations, the adulation of laymen and musicians alike, contribute to his well-being. But his real satisfaction comes from the clinics. With every patient explanation of a point to a student he gives something of himself, and the effects of it are more gratifying than the concert applause. He gives the best that is in him with a forthright and unequivocal stance.

Many people in music believe that Morello's major contribution to music is yet to come—certainly as a teacher and perhaps with his own group. Many possibilities are open to him. Currently, few musicians think of him solely as a jazz drummer; most look upon him as a drum *artist,* because much feeling still exists that he is not really a hard swinger. This may be a carping criticism, but it appears that his work with Brubeck seems to call for just about every kind of playing *but* "hard swinging." There are some good grooves, but the constantly changing, fluctuating rhythms of 5/4, 9/8, and so on (as well as those Dave imposes on the rhythm section in his solos) impede any steady swinging.

When Joe goes "moonlighting" and sits in with different groups (he recently played a set with Dizzy Gillespie and gassed everybody), he is almost like a racehorse that has been allowed to run free after being reined in; and on these occasions he proves again that he can swing strongly when he is among hard-cookers. Then his playing takes on a different quality. It becomes more uninhibited, more relaxed.

A chat with Joe, no matter how it starts, almost invariably ends as a discussion of music in one form or another. Sometimes he gets so wound up that it's more like a filibuster. Never one to hold back, he will animatedly discuss the modern drummer:

> Those things they are playing today . . . Max Roach did that beautifully years ago—Roy Haynes, too (in fact when Bob Carter and I were with you, Marian, we did that same thing—sort of conservatively). But when I see a guy take the butt end of the sticks . . . when I have to guess where the time is, I could cry. Who's going to play against that? Funny—some sixteen-year-olds are digging it! When I was sixteen, I listened to Krupa, Buddy Rich, Max [Roach], Jo Jones.
>
> This whole thing apart, any drummer should be able to play time. These kids coming up . . . they have a choice. Some of them may blow it, but some of them are going to come along and make everybody look like punks.
>
> You know, Marian, you used to say my playing was too precise, but I really think I'm beginning to play more sloppy now. But I'm continually trying to get myself together and play something different, and one thing Dave has taught me—that's to try to create. I admire him harmonically, and you just can't dispute the fact that he plays with imagination. Oh, he's not always the easiest guy to play with, but he's so inventive. . . .
>
> Years ago, I wanted to play like Max, but then I found out you've got to develop your own style . . . good or bad, it's me. But I can't play well all the time—I'm not that consistent. Like, I don't expect to be happy all the time either . . . everyone's been disappointed. But since I've been with Dave, I've had a lot of acclaim, and I'm very grateful for it. Some manifestations of that acclaim have been like dreams come true—you've never dreamed the dreams I've dreamed and had them come true! If I never do more than I have done already, I'm proud and happy for what I've accomplished—God has been good to me.

1965

POSTSCRIPT

I wrote the first of these two articles when Joe Morello was with my trio at the Hickory House and the second after he joined Dave Brubeck.

I've stayed in close touch with Joe, watching him reach greater heights in his profession. Joe Morello today is as fine a player as he ever was, perhaps better, as he has worked in so many different settings after leaving Dave Brubeck—with big bands, in clinics and workshops, and with his own quintet, which he brings together several times a year for club dates in the New Jersey area.

Joe has been teaching ever since I first met him. Even at the Hickory House he would have drummers surrounding him between sets, and now students fly in from all over the country to study with him. He is a patient, painstaking teacher. "I just teach them to play the instrument like [George Lawrence] Stone did with me," he says. "I want to pass along everything he showed me—how to play with any group, to listen to the music, to learn how to leave space."

Joe is as interested and involved in music as ever, and to me his playing has become even more exciting, with his innate use of dynamics, blazing technique, innovative ideas, and off-the-wall humor. He has always had a sense of the ridiculous, and he applies it to the music, adding hip rhythmic touches to four-bar breaks and drum solos.

The last time he sat in with my trio he demonstrated once again his total mastery of the drums and his ability to go from a hard-driving beat to the merest whisper as he switches from sticks to brushes. He knows how to create a mood with a delicate touch on the cymbal, and his interpolations are as sly and quirky as ever. It is good to know that the beat goes on, Morello-style!

In the last couple of years Joe and I have done a few dates together, and it is heartening to know that he is playing as well as ever. I asked Joe and bassist Bill Crow to be a part of the concert being put together for me at Town Hall for my eightieth birthday. A great many of my friends and fellow musicians took part in the concert, but it was especially rewarding to have my old sidekicks with me once again, and we played some of our Hickory House repertoire as if there had not been forty-five years in between!!

And the beat is still going on because Joe is more involved than ever with his teaching, to the extent that he has become the guru of drum teachers. He has taught such notables as Charlie Watts of the Rolling Stones, Carl Palmer of Emerson Lake and Palmer, and other famous sidemen who feel they can learn from him. He has also been translating some of his ideas and techniques into drum instruction books and videos, which not only show his teaching ability and the clear way he expresses himself but also his great sense of humor. The videos are fun to watch, even for a nondrummer like myself!

It's hard to believe that Joe is now over seventy years old, because his spirit is youthful and energetic, and he looks forward to every day of playing with the same interest and intensity as he did years ago. He has put together a new trio and performs in some venues close to his home in New Jersey. Although he is not on the scene as much as he was when he was working with Dave Brubeck, he is known throughout the world as one of the finest drummers extant. I am happy that we are close friends and colleagues, looking forward to more gigs in the future.

 **5**

Perils of Paul:
A Portrait of
Desperate Desmond

A few months from now the Dave Brubeck Quartet will celebrate its tenth anniversary as a unit. Few, if any, jazz groups now playing have endured that long, though the Modern Jazz Quartet is just about the same age. And few have achieved anything even approaching the broad acceptance that the group has found throughout the world.

Today, with a rhythm section comprising Joe Morello on drums and bassist Eugene Wright, the group is, in the opinion of many observers, playing better than ever before. It has not given in to apathy or the repetition of past successes that seem to rob almost all groups of their vitality when they have stayed together too long.

Why?

Undoubtedly a big reason is the tremendous mutual understanding and sympathy—both musical and personal—of Brubeck and his star soloist, alto saxophonist Paul Desmond.

Paul Desmond and Dave Brubeck.

Desmond's status in the group, and in fact in the music business, is unique. With Brubeck, he has all the privileges of a leader, much of the acclaim, and few, if any, of the headaches and responsibilities. It is, as Paul puts it, "a limited partnership." He and Dave consult on choice of tunes, tempos, choruses, and so forth. He also draws a generous percentage of the group's earnings.

"In most groups," Paul says, "if they make it, the leader still goes on paying the same money to the sidemen. So eventually they split like amoebae all over the place. In this case, Dave and I worked out a pretty good arrangement some time ago, and that's the way it's been ever since."

One might assume, therefore, that Paul has a dream job. But on closer look, one is tempted to wonder if, for a man of Paul's talent—in many ways, untapped talent—it might be a gilded cage.

For Desmond has a mind that can only be called brilliant—incredibly quick, perceptive, sensitive. He is also remarkably articulate (his original goal in life was to be a writer not a musician) and witty, with a skill at turning apt and hilarious phrases that leave his friends in hysterics. For example, when a drug company ran an ad for an tranquilizer that showed a bust of composer Richard Wagner (who suffered from splitting headaches) and said that if he'd lived long enough, the new product would have relieved his misery, Desmond promptly dubbed the product "post-Wagnerian anti-drag pills."

Some of his friends are even prone to collecting and quoting Desmondisms, the way in the classical world musicians cherish and repeat the wisecracks of Sir Thomas Beecham.

And his conversation ranges over a vast variety of subjects. Of Jack Kerouac he said, "I hate the way he writes. I kind of like the way he lives, though."

Of *Vogue* fashion models he said, "Sometimes they go around with guys who are scuffling—for a while. But usually they end up marrying some cat with a factory. This is the way the world ends, not with a whim but a banker."

Of yogurt he said, "I don't like it, but Dave is always trying things like that. He's a nutritional masochist. He'll eat anything as long as he figures it's good for him."

And he said (self-revealingly) of contact lenses: "Not for me. If I want to tune everybody out, I just take off my glasses and enjoy the haze."

Other Desmondisms:

Playing funky: "It's kind of a trap. It's easy to do but the mental process involved is self-destructive. After a while it gets difficult to do anything else."

Brigitte Bardot: "That was my favorite thing about playing England—all the girls looked like Brigitte Bardot, and all the guys looked like me."

Cocktail parties: "Depends who's there."

Texas: "No, thanks."

One-nighters: "It's a living."

Yoga: "I could never cross my legs."

He has said about Ornette Coleman:

One thing I'm really against is the tendency for everybody to play like everybody else. You'll hear someone developing and he'll have a definite style of his own, and then you hear him six months later and he sounds like whoever is currently fashionable. There's a lot of submerged individuality which will never appear, I think. That's one thing I like about Ornette. I'm glad he's such an individualist. I like the firmness of thought and purpose that goes into what he's doing, even though I don't always like to listen to it. It's like living in a house where everything's painted red.

And so it goes. Acute perception of life goes on incessantly within Paul and finds its way out in pithy expressions that are only one part of his eloquence. Given so great a versatility (he is also a skillful photographer), such enormous public acceptance, and the respect of a heavy percentage of his fellow musicians, why should Paul not be perpetually blissful?

Alto player Lee Konitz, whose playing has been likened to Desmond's, said recently:

There's an area in Paul that he hasn't been able to realize yet. That's why he gets so depressed—he needs more time to know himself, so that he will get to like himself better. I don't think he has enough time for reflection and thought. I feel that Paul has experienced greatness, and once this feeling of playing what you really hear has been felt by a player, it's difficult to settle for less than this. I feel pretty close to Paul, as I've gone through these things myself, and I still haven't reached the point where I'm happy with what I'm doing.

Paul Emil Breitenfeld ("I picked the name Desmond out of the phone book," he says) was born in San Francisco in 1924. His father played organ for silent movies, wrote band arrangements (and still does), and played accompaniments for vaudeville acts.

As a boy, Paul found family life difficult. When he was five, his mother became ill and he was sent to live with relatives in New Rochelle, New York. In an odd way, his jazz career began there—in grammar school. Paul remembers:

> They had a music period. Like a postgraduate kindergarten band, with psalteries and chimes and all.
>
> By the end of the term I was getting to be like the Terry Gibbs of Daniel Webster School, so they put me down for a solo at one of the assemblies. I was supposed to play one of those grisly semiclassical things. "Dance of the Bridge Trolls" by Glinka, one of those kind of things. Ridiculous. I figured if I just went out and made up something as I went along, it couldn't be any worse. So that's what I did, and it was a gas.
>
> It was the first thing I'd enjoyed doing. (I was kind of a walking vegetable as a kid. Amiable but unfocused.) I didn't realize until about fifteen years later that you could make a living doing this.

Paul returned home to San Francisco in 1936 and started going to Polytechnic High School. "I wanted to learn French, and I was kind of thinking of starting clarinet, but they were both at the same time. So I signed up for French and violin. Dad was very drug when I came home with the program. 'Violin players are a dime a dozen. And French you don't need. Take clarinet.'"

So Paul started studying clarinet—and Spanish. "Which was kind of a drag last year when we went to Paris," he said. "El bombo grande. Well, you can't win 'em all."

Paul played in the school band, edited the school newspaper, and assiduously dodged all forms of exercise. "I discovered early in life that if you take gym first period, you can go into the wrestling room and sit in the corner and sleep."

But it was not until 1943 that Paul began to play alto. That year, he went into the army. For three years he was stationed in San Francisco with the 253rd AGF band: "It was a great way to spend the war. We expected to get shipped out every month, but it never happened. Somewhere in Washington our file must still be on the floor under a desk somewhere."

There were some good local musicians in the band, notably Dave Van Kreidt, a tenor saxophonist and arranger who has been a great friend of Paul's ever since.

One day a friend of Van Kreidt's came through San Francisco. He was a piano player fresh off the ranch, en route overseas as a rifleman and eager to get into the band. His name was Dave Brubeck.

"We had a session in the band room," Paul recalled. "I remember the first tune we played was 'Rosetta.' I was really dazzled by his harmonic approach."

Then, with that expression that tells you you'd better take him with a grain of salt for a moment, Paul said, "I went up to him and said, 'Man, like Wigsville! You really grooved me with those nutty changes.' And Brubeck replied, 'White man speak with forked tongue.'"

Whatever Brubeck and Desmond actually did say to each other, they did not meet again until after the war, when Dave was working around San Francisco, mostly at the Geary Cellar with a group called the Three D's. It was led by a tenor player named Darryl Cutler, and the bass player was Norman Bates. "I went down and sat in, and the musical rapport was very evident and kind of scary. A lot of the things we've done since, we did then, *immediately*—a lot of the counterpoint things, and it really impressed me. If you think Dave plays far out now, you should have heard him then. He made Cecil Taylor sound like Lester Lanin."

Shortly after that, Paul hired Cutler's group away from him—"at some risk of life and limb; Darryl Cutler was a pretty rugged cat"—to work for a few months near Stanford.

> It was a sixty-mile ride and we were making about $50 a night. I was splitting it with the guys and paying for the gas too. That's when I decided I really didn't want to be a leader. A lot of things we did later with the quartet began there.
>
> I've often wondered what would have happened if we'd been in New York at the time—whether it was really as good as I think it was. I have a memory of several nights that seemed fantastic, and I don't

feel that way too often. I'd give anything for a tape of one of those nights now, just to see what was really going on.

I know we were playing a lot of counterpoint on almost every tune, and the general level was a lot more loud, emotional, and unsubtle then. I was always screaming away at the top of the horn, and Dave would be constructing something behind me in three keys. Sometimes I had to plead with him to play something more simple behind me.

It seemed pretty wild at the time; it was one of those few jobs where you really hated to stop—we'd keep playing on the theme until they practically threw us off the stand.

Anyway, that's where the empathy between Dave and me began, and it's survived a remarkable amount of pulling and pushing in the eleven or so years since.

Then the Dave Brubeck Octet started, mainly as a Saturday afternoon rehearsal group for the guys studying composition with Darius Milhaud (Brubeck, Van Kreidt, Bill Smith, Dick Collins, and Jack Weeks). I was the only musical illiterate with that group—I *wasn't* studying with Milhaud.

I was going to San Francisco State College, studying to be a writer. It was the only major where you could get credit for anything you felt like taking—play-writing, social dancing, basket-weaving, anything. I finally decided writing was like playing jazz—it can be learned, but not taught.

The social dancing was kind of wild, though, a sort of Arthur Murray for misfits. The girls were all sort of thin and six feet tall, and the guys were mostly scrawny with glasses like ice-cubes. We met twice a week in the basement of a Greek church near the school, and they had a hand-wound phonograph and about three records. I don't know how old they were, but on one of them, before the music started, you could hear a voice saying, "What hath God wrought?"

Time slipped by, and all of a sudden it was June 1950. "My only jobs had been two concerts with the octet and a Mexican wedding," Paul said. So he decided to take a job with Jack Fina's band. The job got him to New York, with plans in his head to leave the band and go on from there.

But when I arrived in New York, all that happened was that all the guys I talked to wanted my job with Fina, which was pretty discouraging.

Meantime, back at the ranch, Brubeck had started the trio with the advice and support of our patron saint, Jimmy Lyons (then a disc jockey, now manager of the Monterey Jazz Festival). Dave had also started his own record company, which was really a hurdle back in those pre-LP days. So I went back to San Francisco and stayed there for a while with my nose pressed firmly to the window, and in 1951 we started the quartet.

Even then Paul had a kind of veneration for Brubeck, compounded of affection, admiration, and respect. In answer to the oft-made observation that "Dave never would have made it without Paul Desmond," Paul says:

> *I* would never have made it without *Dave.* He's amazing harmonically, and he can be a fantastic accompanist. You can play the wrongest note, possible in any chord, and he can make it sound like the only right one.
>
> I still feel more kinship musically with Dave than with anyone else, although it may not always be evident. But when he's at his best, it's really something to hear. A lot of people don't know this, because in addition to the kind of fluctuating level of performance that most jazz musicians give, Dave has a real aversion to working things out, and a tendency to take the things he *can* do for granted and spend most of his time trying to do other things. This is okay for people who have heard him play at his best, but sometimes mystifying to those who haven't.
>
> However, once in a while somebody who had no use for Dave previously comes in and catches a really good set and leaves looking kind of dazed.

Because of his affection for Brubeck, Paul feels it sharply when his friend is criticized. And the Brubeck group has run into perhaps more than its fair share of criticism. Yet Paul usually gets off unscathed. Ira Gitler recently wrote a stinging review of a new quartet record. Yet he said: "Paul Desmond's playing is another proof that jazz has many shades of expression, that you can communicate deep emotion without histrionics. However, I'd like to hear him play a set with Al Cohn and Zoot Sims; I think it would prove stimulating."

And, though Desmond has characterized himself as the "disembodied saxophonist of the Brubeck group," John S. Wilson wrote after the group's performance this year at Newport: "Desmond seems to be the bellwether of the . . . quartet. When he is uninspired, the entire group is affected, largely because Brubeck seems to push harder, bringing out the worst side of his playing. But when Paul is at the top of his form, Dave really relaxes."

Desmond seems to command an enormous amount of respect among fellow musicians, though by no means all of them. Miles Davis, who has put down a good many of his fellow artists, has said loftily, "I just don't like the sound of an alto played that way."

More specific in his criticism was alto saxophonist Jackie McLean: "Desmond's playing is pleasant—progressive—but not particularly moving to me. As far as technique is concerned, he has wonderful control of his instrument. But then, so has Dick Stabile. I feel that his playing is sort of a launching pad for Dave's music. But it's very lyrical, he plays good ideas, and they are his own ideas."

But Julian "Cannonball" Adderley—who is Paul's arch-competitor for top alto spot in the various polls, most of which Paul has won in recent years—said, "I believe that Paul Desmond shares with Benny Carter the title of most lyrical altoist. He is a profoundly beautiful player." Sonny Stitt, another of today's top altoists, said, "He plays good music. He's not on Cloud 9 all the time, like some of those guys. I like him very much."

And Dizzy Gillespie, a sort of father figure for a great many of today's jazzmen, said: "Paul and Dave sure do something for one another. The ideas that Paul gets are in the same groove as Dave's. They seem to have terrific rapport. It takes a lot to get such cohesion between two people in a unit."

Perhaps the best appraisal of Paul Desmond and his music comes from the man who knows both better than anyone else—Dave Brubeck.

> I've heard him play more than anyone else has, and even after all these years, he still surprises me. There are so many imitators of Charlie Parker, and to me Paul is one of the few true individuals on his instrument. Musicians will put one idol before them and think that everything should revolve around this person and that everyone should play *his* way—and this curbs individuality.
>
> Paul's big contribution is going to be that he *didn't* copy Charlie Parker.
>
> I believe that Paul and I make a good team. We've had many conflicts and we will probably have many more, but there are a lot of things we haven't done yet and can do if we can stick together and put up with each other.

Yet even though Paul finds his association with Dave so satisfying (and vice versa), there are constant if subtle pressures on the altoist to strike out on his own. Desmond has made notably few recordings with anyone but Brubeck, leading many musicians to wonder—like critic Gitler—how he would sound in another context.

Of those few discs has made with others (Gerry Mulligan, Don Elliott), his favorite is one made recently for the Warner Bros. label. Working with him were Percy Heath, Connie Kay, and Jim Hall. Though suspicions are occasionally voiced that anyone who has been a sideman for ten years would run into difficulty as leader, guitarist Hall's comments on the date would tend to indicate the contrary.

> I learned a lot about Paul, due to the fact that each of us had to give a high-level performance at the same time as the other fellow. I was very impressed with his musicianship, especially his ability to play a long melody line through a series of choruses. We made several takes, and every one of *his* takes was almost perfect; *we* were the ones who messed up.
>
> But aside from the music, he's such a charming guy, and though he may not be forceful in the same way some musicians are, I know

that he knows what he wants from a group. He may not stomp and shout, but he gets things done just the same.

Paul continues to have the same lack of enthusiasm for leadership that he did when he hired the Darryl Cutler group away and tried the role for a while.

But the time may come when he will give in.

I guess it's inevitable that I'll have my own group one of these days, if for no other reason than that Dave will probably wander off into other fields and not do as much playing as he's doing now.

The problem then will be to find guys I can communicate with musically and get along with the rest of the time. The ideal, for me, is a group with a lot of cooperative playing going on, as opposed to a procession of virtuosi, if that's the word I want. Guys who can improve together in such a way that the whole turns out to be greater than the sum of all the parts. I have that feeling with Dave a lot, which is one reason I've hung around this long, also with Gerry Mulligan and Jim Hall.

Finding the right guys, I think, is really the hardest part of being leader. The rest gets to be largely routine and resigning yourself to being a bad guy part of the time. And a certain amount of patience, fortitude, and delicate negotiation is necessary even for "illustrious" sidemen like me.

Whether or not he does strike out as a leader, however, Paul has more than enough to keep him occupied—or preoccupied as the case may be. He is pursuing his own musical ideal, and his distinctive sound—light, liquid, at times mournful—will continue to be an important voice in jazz.

I love the way Miles plays. I still think the hardest thing of all to do is to come up with things that are simple, melodic, and yet new. Until fairly recently, most of the landmarks in jazz history could be written out and played by practically anybody after they had been done. It just took a long time for them to be thought of. There's a lot more going on now in terms of complexity, but it's still a long time between steps.

Complexity can get to be a trap, too. I think it gets to be more fun to play than to listen to. You can have a ball developing a phrase, inverting it, playing it in different keys and times and all. But it's really more introspective than communicative. Like a crossword puzzle compared to a poem.

What would kill me the most on the jazz scene these days would be for everybody to go off in a corner and sound like himself. Let a hundred flowers bloom. Diversitysville. There's enough conformity in the rest of this country without having it prevail in jazz, too.

I should mention in connection with anything critical I say about anyone else that about 80 percent of the things I play I hate to listen to afterwards. I kind of know what I'd like to be doing ultimately on the horn, but it's hard to make any progress while you're traveling. Hard enough even in one place, as far as that goes.

But the things I'm after musically are clarity, emotional communication on a not-too-obvious level, the kind of form in a chorus that doesn't hit you over the head but is there if you look for it, humor, and construction that sounds logical in an unexpected way.

That and a good, dependable high F-sharp and I'll be happy.

1960

POSTSCRIPT

This article was written while I was at the Hickory House, when Paul and Dave Brubeck had already garnered some recognition but had not yet reached the peak they would attain when Joe Morello and Gene Wright joined the quartet.

I have fond memories of Paul, and they were especially vivid when I went to hear music at Bradley's (alas, no longer in existence). Paul left his Steinway grand piano to Bradley Cunningham for his club. This was so typical of Paul—he loved the club and spent a lot of time there, listening to the music, sitting in, and fraternizing with his many friends. I got to play on the piano myself on many occasions; I only regret that Paul and I never played together. He used to come to hear me at the Carlyle Hotel, and he always promised to sit in, but he never did.

Alec Wilder and I often ran into Paul when we were dining at the French Shack. Paul lived in the apartment building next door and ate in the restaurant almost every night. Alec admired Paul greatly and would always ask him to join us. He usually did, even though he always arrived armed with a book and sat alone in a far corner (much as Alec himself would do on occasion). Paul and Alec would always launch into brilliant, witty conversation, and I would try to put in my two cents' worth whenever they paused for breath.

Not everyone knows that the most successful of Dave Brubeck's recorded hits, "Take Five," was written by Paul. This tune has been absorbed into the jazz, pop, and even Musak repertoire. It's the most popular jazz tune written in 5/4 time and has become universally known. It's sad Paul is not here to enjoy its continued commercial success. The song is clever, sophisticated, and humorous, rather like Paul himself.

I remember calling Paul in the hospital when I heard he was ill. He sounded very cheerful, but as we chatted I heard the click of a cigarette lighter. I said, "Are you still smoking?" "Yes, why not?" he said. I couldn't answer. It became apparent that Paul was determined to live out the rest of his life the way he always had—drinking, smoking, enjoying the company of friends, hanging out at Elaine's, going to hear music, and occasionally playing. His last appearance was with Dave Brubeck at Avery Fisher Hall in 1979. By then he was thin and pale, but he played with the same beautiful tone quality and inventiveness as he always had, leaving a lasting and memorable testimony to his unique talent.

Paul Desmond is still very much in our collective memories. No one else has ever managed to duplicate his melodic ideas and the tranquil beauty of his sound. It is ironic that since he wrote "Take Five" it has become the most popular tune in Dave Brubeck's repertoire, but now it has been stretched into all kinds of twisted variations, many of which are heard on commercial radio or "smooth jazz" stations. I'm sure Paul would make some caustic remark if he heard that the tune he had so aptly called "Take Five" is now being played in 4/4 time and with terrible lyrics! However, I'm sure that Dave Brubeck is not complaining, as his company publishes the song! We all miss Paul—his humor, his exquisite sound, his sometimes quirky but often delightful personality. He will never be forgotten.

Into the Sun:
An Affectionate Sketch
of Mary Lou Williams

Her early records are collector's items. Her writing and playing have become part of the pattern of jazz history. She has transcended the difficulties experienced by women in the music field and through several decades has held a position of eminence as one of the most original and creative of pianists. She speaks softly: "Anything you are shows up in your music—jazz is whatever *you* are, playing yourself, being yourself, letting your thoughts come through."

Her voice has the ring of authority, and well it may, for Mary Lou Williams's career, dating back to her childhood in Pittsburgh, Pennsylvania, and her Kansas City days with the Andy Kirk Orchestra, has always been one of consistent musical integrity.

Mary Lou's playing is real. Earthy. Running through all the emotions, it speaks volumes, for there is much in its creator that comes out in the music, a part of herself she cannot help revealing, so that at times

Mary Lou Williams.

one has the feeling almost of intruding on her thoughts, of hearing se-
crets not meant to be shared, of being able to probe the recesses of her
mind. Sometimes Mary Lou's mood is dark, brooding—like a pearl div-
er, she searches along the depths of the lower register of the piano and
then, as if triumphant at a sudden discovery, she shifts to the treble,
launching into a series of light, pulsating, chordal figures.

She possesses a natural ability to generate a swinging feeling—an
infallible time sense—an original harmonic concept, a way of voicing
chords that is hers alone. She doesn't veer far from the blues. Whatever
her mood, whatever the tempo, she weaves a pattern, a design, faint at
first, like a rubbed drawing, but then appearing more strongly until it
breaks into a kaleidoscope of color.

Mary Lou has found the way to put her emotions, thoughts, and feelings to good use. They come out powerfully and sometimes prayerfully,
for the spiritual side of the blues is always strong in her work. Yet there

is a mysterious air, an enigmatic, slightly feline quality about her, which contrasts strangely with her direct, down-to-earth way of speaking.

"Anything you are shows up in your music."

One senses the inner fires, the inner tensions, and though she keeps her voice low at times there is in it a note of bitterness. She has none of the typical trappings of show business. She seems almost indifferent to her appearance, her hair brushed casually, her dress plain and unassuming, her only jewelry a gold cross on a chain. But Mary Lou Williams is not a plain woman; with her high cheek bones, reminiscent of the Mayans, she is beautiful. When she becomes involved in her music, her face will set in masklike concentration, her eyes closed, giving an impression of stillness, of being lost to the world, even though her foot is tapping and her strong hands are moving swiftly and surely over the keys. Then suddenly she opens her eyes and smiles, and her face lights up and reflects her spirit, her gaiety, and her lively sense of humor.

A religious woman, Miss Williams was introduced to Roman Catholicism several years ago, along with Dizzy Gillespie's wife, Lorraine (the Gillespies have long been her staunch friends), and it has evidently given her new strength and courage and a fresh purpose. Mary Lou is ready to do battle with the specters of the past. Strong in her faith, strong in her beliefs, a woman with a cause, a crusader, she rails against the injustices of a materialistic world and deplores musicians talking against each other more than they help each other. Yet she has seemed to have had difficulty finding herself, too. In a sense, she is like a child who dreams of a good and perfect world and cannot quite tolerate the fact that it isn't that way.

At the Hickory House, where she has been ensconced for the last several months, the ebb and flow of noise in the room blurs her intricately voiced harmonies and dulls the impact of her changes in dynamics, making even more desirable the seats at the bar close to the piano where one can almost shut out the noise of the room and concentrate on Mary Lou and her trio. She sits at the piano with a certain dignity, playing with pride and a sureness of touch. Hers is a natural showmanship, complete involvement with the music that speaks for her. But still one must listen closely to get the message.

"Anything you are shows up in your music."

Here is a woman who is conscientious, introspective, sensitive, a woman who, with her quiet manner and at times almost brusque, noncommittal way of speaking, has been misunderstood, thought to be lacking in warmth and compassion. The reverse is true. She feels keenly the various factions, contradictions, inequalities of the music business, wants to help people, to give of herself. A woman vulnerable. A woman hurt so many times she tends to withdraw from, and be suspicious of, others unless she knows them well. She has an uncanny way of stripping them of any facade, of cutting through the deceit and shallowness of the sycophants. In many ways she is still confused, still searching, still figuring things out for herself, and in this she has been helped a great deal by her friend, the Reverend Anthony Woods.

"She has the beauty of being simple without any affectation—simplicity with her is a very deep thing," Father Woods said. "I have heard her discuss the esthetics of music with great penetration. She seems to have an understanding of what is good, of what is beautiful. She thinks that jazz is becoming superficial, that it's losing its spiritual feeling. She seems to be aware of a great deal of falsity and affectation, that people are not telling the truth, not saying what they really mean. In her uncomplicated way she can't understand how anybody can't be sincere.

"To me, she is one of the greatest persons I have ever met—really a very great soul. She has exquisite taste, and where there is goodness, she gravitates to it naturally. But she is an emotional thinker, a disorganized thinker, and sometimes she has to sort out her ideas, and that's where I come in. She's simple and direct, primitive in a very good sense, and not spoiled by the sophistication around her. I don't believe that Mary is capable of producing anything except what is good."

Mary Lou has little business ability and scant knowledge of how to correlate, to direct, her ideas and plans. But her dreams and wishes for the betterment of musicians are logical and sound, and now some of them are just beginning to come true.

Several years ago she started a thrift shop, the proceeds from which go into her Bel Canto Foundation, which she established to help needy musicians. Now more and more people have begun to hear about it and are giving her gifts of clothing and other donations. Besides these activities, much of Mary Lou's time is taken up with writing and arranging plus her daily attendance at mass and care of her sister's little boy, who usually has the run of her apartment.

Being so busy does not seem to faze her, but it has been a long time since she has "come out" to play in public. She has made a few sporadic appearances in the last few years—twice at New York City's Wells' Supper Club and once each at The Embers and The Composer (where I worked opposite her), plus the Palace Hotel in San Francisco. These engagements have been of short duration and have not been too satisfying to her. She seems to feel the pressures of a musician's life keenly, to become disillusioned, and then, as she expresses it, "goes back in"— back to her other world, to her apartment, to write, teach, and pray.

During her long stays at home, Mary Lou's talent certainly has not been lying fallow. She has composed a poignant minor blues she calls "Dirge Blues," which she wrote at the time of President John F. Kennedy's assassination. She is skillful in creating a mood—the feeling of this piece is tragic and gloomy. In its simplicity it is very touching. She has put out an extended-play record on her own label, Mary Records, consisting of three tunes arranged for sixteen voices and her trio: "Summertime," "The Devil," and "St. Martin dePorres." The last tune, with a lyric by Father Woods, achieves an airy, ethereal quality by its voice blending. She has made a single, also on her own label, of "My Blue Heaven." She makes this warhorse like new again, with a light, witty, Latin-based treatment. Obviously she has lost none of her powers of inventiveness. One has only to listen to her recordings of years ago— "Froggy Bottom," "Roll 'Em," and "Cloudy"—to realize how her style has evolved with the years and how she has kept her playing and her thinking contemporary.

She composed one of the first (if not the first) jazz waltzes—"Mary's Waltz"—many years ago, yet she has never got the proper credit or recognition for this or for any of her several innovations that have been brought to the fore later by other musicians. Her importance, her influence, cannot be denied. She has written many beautiful tunes that are seldom heard, seldom recorded.

It has been said of Mary Lou Williams that she plays in clichés, but she has so much to offer of her own that I feel that her occasional use of cliché is more tongue-in-cheek commentary than lack of inventiveness. She has been labeled by some a fanatic. To others, she is only an extremely dedicated musician. Yet perhaps there *is* something of the fanatic in her, as seen in her constant search for musicians with whom she can be compatible—in a way she reminds one of a mother with her children, alternately scolding or praising them, trying to teach them, trying to instill her beliefs in them, expecting great things of them. Yet it is said too that she is a hard taskmistress, demanding and intolerant.

"Anything you are shows up in your music."

Her feelings about the new freedom in jazz cannot quite be concealed, though she tries to be noncommittal.

"I just haven't got it figured out," she said. "To each his own, I guess, but if I can't hear chords . . . some sort of melody . . . well, if they think they're giving out a good sound, that's their business. Maybe they think we're squares? Or else it's some sort of protest? Take a guy like Coltrane, he knows what he's doing, but these people without a knowledge of music, it's like—well, it's a very neurotic world. People are nervous. Seems like everyone I know is nervous. It must be the pressures of the world. Musicians are very sensitive, and they really don't know what to do about it. I don't mean they're nervous about playing, but in their lives. I try to act relaxed because that's been my training, but I'm more nervous than anyone you ever knew—inside. Oh, I get mad, sometimes, but I expel it, get it out right away."

When one is discussing Mary Lou with other musicians, her sense of time always prompts admiration.

"I've heard her a few times at the Hickory House, and I'm amazed at her rhythmic approach more than anything else," said fellow pianist Billy Taylor.

She has the most consistent way of swinging; even with a rhythm section that isn't quite hanging together, she can make it swing, and this is really remarkable. It seems that no matter what's going on around her, she can get this thing going. When in doubt—swing! As a pianist, I naturally listen a lot to the rhythm section, and sometimes I'll notice that they're not together, and I'll think to myself, "Come on!—let's give her some support," but she'll be making it anyway. Not as many jazz pianists have this ability as do other instrumentalists, I mean this rhythmic propulsion. She's not like an Erroll Garner or an Oscar Peterson, who overpower the rhythm section. On the contrary, she plays so subtly she seems to be able to isolate herself and swing, though the others may not be. Considering all the psychological things that go into swinging, she's even more remarkable. You could wake her up out of a dead sleep, and she'd start swinging without even thinking about it.

Mary Lou is looking for perfection. On the rare occasions when she has had this chemical thing going that can happen between three people, she's been so excited by it that she wants it all the time. Swinging is so natural to her that she can't understand why it isn't necessarily natural to everybody all the time. She figures that they can do it, but they won't; she thinks to herself, "Anybody I hire should be able to do this, so why don't they?" Most people associate the verb "to swing" with the degree of loudness that they attain, but she refutes it—she'll take something pianissimo and swing just as hard as if it were double forte. She's one of the few people I know that can do this, consistently swing in any context.

"Anything you are shows up in your music."

"She lives in a world all her own, a dream world, and she doesn't want anything to spoil it," said her longtime friend and admirer, Hickory House press agent Joe Morgen.

She inspires a great devotion in people—she has many followers, but there are just as many people who look at her askance because they cannot understand her high artistic level. She is so dedicated, and the fact that her standards are high makes her very hard to please. In her accompaniment she wants to hear certain changes behind her, certain lines, certain rhythms, and it's difficult for a strongly individualistic bass player or drummer, with ideas of his own, to conform to her standards. But her motive, her burning desire is for creation. In a way, she's like a little child with a doll house, setting up house in the piano, like a little girl on her own chair, not even thinking about what is going on around her. Sometimes she doesn't hear what you're saying—doesn't even see you—because her mind is a million miles away. People don't understand that if she doesn't speak to them, she doesn't mean to be rude.

Mary Lou herself said, "When people tell me that I'm playing good, and I don't think I am, I want to run away from them, not speak to them."

Being so intensely self-critical, she has scant regard for musicians who, in her opinion, lack sufficient dedication to their instruments.

"So many musicians nowadays push too hard, spread themselves too thin, doing all kinds of things when they should be home practicing," she said. "People who push that hard never really get anywhere, but if you know your instrument, well, you can lay back and let someone pick you out. If you're doing too many things, there's no chance for your creativeness to come through.

"When the rhythm section starts composing things on the stand, they'll push me into composing. But if they are not together, you must let them walk, let them play by themselves, to find out where they are. Then when they're really tight, you come in and play. But if they're still not making it, then play another tune, play a ballad. When you hear me play chimes, it's because the rhythm isn't right, and you've got to bring a section together to let them hear themselves. But if, after this, they still don't make it, then I'll start cussing!

"Now that I'm out here, I'm beginning to like it. I haven't been late for the job, and I haven't wanted to leave, and that's unusual for me.

Sometimes in the past, I've got fed up, and I would walk out and say, 'You better get yourself another piano player.' But this time it's fun for me. Sometimes I'm tired, but I haven't had that feeling of wanting to give up. . . . I think this time that I'm out here to stay."

It is almost as if she sees herself emerging from darkness into the sunlight to bask in the warmth of feeling generated by friends, admirers, and family. Gazing out over the piano, her pleasure in playing comes through clearly.

1966

POSTSCRIPT

If Mary Lou were alive today she would still be moving ahead in her playing, writing, and harmonic ideas. I often feel a twinge of sadness because her music is not often heard and is appreciated mainly by jazz aficionados while puerile songs have all but taken over the music scene.

Mary Lou was fearless—she even took on Cecil Taylor in a duo concert at Carnegie Hall. And she was feisty. She was fond of saying, "I play like a man, but I'm very feminine." Yet one didn't often see that side of her in later years. She could be very stern, somewhat curt and strict with her sidemen, often telling them what to play. She sometimes hired musicians who were inexperienced, and she seemed to enjoy training them—calling out the notes she wanted to hear and growling, "Play them changes."

Later in her career she often would say that there was no love in the jazz world, yet perhaps without realizing it she expressed great love through her music, and she gave of herself in many ways. In 1977 she was offered a position on the music faculty at Duke University, where she spent the last years of her life conducting classes, writing, arranging, and working with students. It seemed fitting for Mary Lou to be at Duke. Her position on the faculty brought her into a first-rate musical situation, worthy of her great talent. She bought a house in Durham, North Carolina, and seemed happier and more settled than she ever had been before. A few years previously Mary Lou had met an energetic and enthusiastic young Jesuit priest, Father Peter O'Brien, who was devoted to her. He helped her with her various activities, handling her bookings and assisting her with her work at Duke. When she was taken ill with the cancer that finally caused her death, she bore it bravely, with the fortitude and strength of will she had shown throughout her life. She continued to write arrangements and meet with her music class, stalwart to the end. She imbued the students with her principles, her rules for good playing, her constant search for fresh ideas, and her musical integrity. We are fortunate that these young musicians are carrying on the tradition she left behind.

A few years ago I decided to record some of Mary Lou's music because I felt that many of her tunes were not getting enough exposure. Some of them are extensions of the blues, and they have beautiful melodies that are great vehicles for improvisation. Mary Lou's writing shows that she was really ahead of her time. Her use of harmony was sometimes very complex and strange. Two years ago, I thought how wonderful it would be to perform her *Mass for Peace.* The Mass was written many years ago and had been performed in some schools and colleges, but to my way of thinking it had never received the proper treatment. I got in touch with my friend Mary Ann Brownlow in Washington, D.C., who had a connection to the Washington National Cathedral. I also called Mary Lou's longtime manager and keeper of her archives, Father Peter O'Brien. He was very enthusiastic about the idea and was able to produce all the necessary music for the choir and the musicians. It was wonderful to see how a dream could so easily become a reality. Actually, it took more than a year to organize the event, but in March 1999 there we were, rehearsing the music with not one but two choirs—the Eastern High School Choir, directed by Joyce Garrett, and the Cathedral Choir. We had piano, bass, drums, guitar, and French horn. Our conductor was Dr. David Baker from Indiana University. I found some of the music very challenging; in fact, there were a couple of pieces that I really couldn't play, and I asked the pianist from the Cathedral to take over for me. All in all, the performance was a great success. The Cathedral was packed, and the whole concert was recorded for National Public Radio. I think Mary Lou would have been pleased with the way things went. We got rave reviews, and the Mass has been broadcast several times on NPR. Now we are thinking of the possibility of doing another performance because we all know so much more about the music and how exciting and dramatic it is. This may well be a project that will come to fruition in the next year or so.

Mary Lou would also be happy to see that there is now a yearly jazz festival in her name in Washington, D.C., featuring women players: the

Mary Lou Williams Jazz Festival at the Kennedy Center. Some of the younger players may not know too much about Mary Lou's history, but they certainly are learning about it now, and one hopes that more of her music will be performed as part of the jazz repertoire.

Mary Lou Williams is finally getting some of the recognition she so richly deserves.

Just Swinging:
Jake Hanna

As a youngster, Jake Hanna had three idols—Brace Beemer (radio's Lone Ranger), Benny Goodman, and Ted Williams. "Brace Beemer disappeared from the scene, Ted Williams has retired, and when I auditioned for Benny, he didn't dig me—now I'm all alone," Jake said in his joking, nonchalant way.

Jake is, in a sense, alone, inasmuch as he is almost without peer in his particular field as a big-band drummer. He has been with the Woody Herman Band for almost two years now, and his hard-driving, unabashed, exciting playing has been a major contribution to the renewed popularity of the band.

In the last few years Jake has been moving from one band or small group to another and back again. He has been with Maynard Ferguson three times, twice with my trio, at least three times with Japanese pianist Toshiko Akiyoshi Mariano, twice before with Herman, and in between there have been short stints with Ted Weems, Buddy Morrow, Herb Pomeroy, Bobby Hackett, Duke Ellington, and Harry James.

If all this were not enough to make him a well-rounded player, he also has been the house drummer at George Wein's Storyville during return visits to his home town of Dorchester, Massachusetts, a suburb of Boston, backing such varied stylists as Buck Clayton, Jimmy Rushing, and Anita O'Day. Now he appears to have achieved his happiest groove with the Herman band.

His work with different groups has enabled him to experiment and to learn by trial and error what to do and what not to do in varying circumstances, and now he is bringing the results of these experiences to bear in the masterful handling of his current job.

There is an easy flow, a logical, methodical purpose, to everything Jake does. Undoubtedly he is following established patterns set down by former Herman drummers Dave Tough and Don Lamond, and he draws inspiration from their ideas and from those of his idols Buddy Rich and Jo Jones, not consciously copying them but nevertheless revealing that these are his influences while adding to them his unique personality, imagination, and humor. He is a pleasure to watch; there is no wasted motion yet he is a flamboyant performer who does everything with a flourish and a jaunty, good-natured air. He uses his technique logically—no unnecessary pyrotechnics—and he has the good judgment and the power necessary to hold and control the rhythm at all times.

To many listeners the Herman band is more exciting now than it has ever been.

"We could never play such up-tempo things before," Herman said. "None of the other drummers I have had would attempt these frantic tempos. Now I can show off the band more—it all makes for a lot of excitement—something added that we couldn't do fifteen years ago, and it is challenge to the musicians to play when they know they can feel comfortable. Everything's easy, no pressure."

Yet as hard as Jake can drive a big band, he can be subtle with a small group, a sympathetic and sensitive player creating a tremendously swinging feeling and a comfortable, easy groove.

Perhaps "comfortable" is the key word to his playing. It reflects his personality and his approach to music, for he is an easygoing bachelor of thirty-two, a convivial soul who enjoys the hurly-burly of musicians' hangouts in his free time. He makes the rounds of clubs where his friends are working and, whenever the opportunity presents itself, likes to sit in. He is a musician in the true sense, totally involved with playing, discussing music, and listening to it, and he is one of the most completely cheerful people one could meet. Though he affects a bluff air and a joking, irreverent attitude toward most things, he is still sincere, dedicated, and honest.

Jake's musical education dates back to his school days in Roxbury, Massachusetts, where at eight he started to play drums with the church band.

"I still play in that same vein too," he said. "Sort of a marching feeling—two-bar phrases."

Later, with his older brother and two sisters, he attended Dorchester High School, where he played in the school band, and whenever he had the chance he would go to the RKO Theater to listen to the big bands that came through town periodically. He fell under the joint influence of Buddy Rich, who was then with Tommy Dorsey, and Gene Krupa.

"When I heard 'Sing, Sing, Sing,' I decided that I wanted to be that kind of drummer—but then I started to dig Jo Jones and Dave Tough. This was a big enlightenment to me. I had no idea drums could be played this way, and I was able to absorb the style firsthand, because my brother was playing drums at the time and he would play the cymbal beat a lot like Dave did. (My brother was 4-F so he was getting all the work.)"

At eighteen, Jake was starting to get gigs around Boston and was sitting in when he could. However, the long arm of the draft board soon reached out to take him from his comfortable home in Dorchester and deposit him in the Air Force base in San Antonio, Texas, where he was stationed for the next three and one-half years, playing bass drums in an Air Force band.

"When I got out, I was stranded in Texas," Jake said ruefully. "Then Tommy Reed offered me a gig and saved me. I only had four bucks to my name, so he sent me $9 for the bus fare to Shreveport, Louisiana, to join the band. (Come to think of it my salary wasn't much more than that bus fare.) I went with Tommy for two weeks but wound up staying for over a year."

When Jake left the band in Kansas City, Kansas, he returned to Boston and started playing with local groups again and studying drums with Stanley Spector. Jake gives Spector, with whom he studied for three years (and has on and off since), all the credit for his background and for his proficiency.

"There is no other teacher for me," he declared. "Many of them are so busy with the hands, building technique. Having 'good hands' has nothing to do with playing jazz. I am sure Buddy Rich and Joe Morello would still be as great if they didn't have 'good hands.' You've got to do first things first—learn to keep time and swing—the basic things a drummer is supposed to do, but you can't just do it right off the bat; it takes a while."

During the next three years Jake studied and practiced, meanwhile working with various groups, including Morrow's, Weems's, and Toshiko's, who was at that time at the Berklee School of Music in Boston. In 1958 he went with Ferguson for several months, and in 1959 wound up back in Boston playing at Storyville behind Clayton and Rushing.

"I finally got the message at that point," Jake said. "Suddenly I knew that that was the style I sound best in. No confusion—everything very simple. Basic."

It was then that I really began to be aware of Jake's playing, although I had heard him previously at the Hickory House with Toshiko and had met him there. I was in Boston at the time he was backing Anita O'Day at Storyville. Anita invited me to sit in. I did so, and I was tremendously excited by the immediate rapport between Jake and myself and by the easy, relaxed feeling he created. I asked him to join my group, which he did shortly thereafter, working with me for the next two years.

The enjoyment of this period was interrupted only once, when Jake (who is now well known for giving little or no notice when he decides to leave a band) elected to go back to Boston to work with the Herb Pomeroy Band. Being the diplomat he is, he handed me his notice—and a parting gift of a Waring Blendor—simultaneously. He returned after a few weeks, however, to join me at the Hickory House, where, with Ben Tucker on bass, we spent one of the swingingest summers I have ever known.

Then Jake became impatient to try another groove, and he left, this time for good, to join Bobby Hackett at Eddie Condon's club, where for a while he slipped into a different musical genre, a Dixieland-ish kick in which he is as much at ease as he is with other styles of playing.

After a few months he took off again, this time to join the Duke Ellington Band, spelling Sam Woodyard for a short stint.

Of this adventure, Jake said, "I went along to hear the music from the middle of the band—best seat in the house. That's why I never sounded good with those guys. I was too busy listening! Now *there's* the greatest reed section in all history—great band, great time."

During the summer of 1961 Jake went to Jacksonville, Florida, with Ross Tompkin's trio and on his return was invited to join Harry James's band in Las Vegas, Nevada. After a few weeks, it appeared that the drummer–leader relationship was somewhat less than euphoric, and Jake quit the band and soon returned to the Herman Herd for the third time.

Nowadays many up-and-coming drummers are preoccupied with the "new thing," employing complicated rhythmic patterns and cross-rhythms that scatter around the instrumentalists like gunfire. They flay the drums as if they were a team of recalcitrant horses. To some of them Jake's playing is considered old-fashioned, but their opinions and their asserted striving toward greater freedom leave him cold.

"To me freedom is gained through *limiting* your playing, disciplining yourself," Jake said. "Some modern drummers don't play with license. They play free, but they lose the feeling of freedom by their irre-sponsibility. Jazz is a real paradox—you have to hold the sticks tight in order to play loose, and the less you play the more comes out! With these new guys, they keep puttin' in all the time, and when you've got to play against that stuff, it's rough. To them, phrasing is shifting the rhythm back and forth all the time. There's too much going on, and usually it's too loud. Drummers are like the line on a football team—they're there at all times . . . dependable . . . but they are not supposed to be heroes.

"I don't think jazz will ever hit that real happy groove again unless drummers go back to swinging the time, not shifting it around. Now, there's one guy who is a master of that style, and I really dig his playing—that's Roy Haynes. He has finesse, taste. And taste is the hardest thing to learn—you've got to know how to balance up the drum set, how to get an even sound, and most of all know what to leave out. That's why I dig Gus Johnson; so little goes in, so much comes out. Jo Jones, Shelly Manne, Don Lamond—they're great. To me, Shelly is a jazz version of Billy Gladstone, and he was the supreme artist. (You know, Billy practi-cally brought up Shelly—used to wheel him around in the baby car-riage.)"

It is evident that Jake has strong opinions, and he likes to air them. He believes in what he is doing and makes no bones about it. He is sure of his playing, and though to some he may seem at times overconfident, his sense of humor saves him from offensiveness—and he can fulfill any musical demands made on him.

He always seems able to play at the top of his form and to engender a good feeling among the people around him. As a person and as a mu-sician he wears well.

Herman is as pleased to have Jake back with the band as Jake is to be there. "Since he was with me three or four years ago his playing has changed tremendously," Herman said. "It's like night and day. Ninety-nine-and-a-half percent of the time he is absolutely right with every-thing he does. The truly important members of the band are drums and lead trumpet. If they are not right, forget it. Jake is the first *great* big-band drummer to come along since Dave Tough and Don Lamond. He deserves the high praise he is getting."

Jake is happy, he says, with the way things are shaping up. His philosophy of life is characteristically humorous and simple: "I guess you have to roll with the punches—keep bobbing and weaving . . . maybe throw a couple now and then. Life is a fight, and naturally I don't want to get wasted. So I take things as they come. Nice and easy."

When working at New York's Metropole, where the Herman band often plays, the musicians have to stand in a single line along a platform that runs practically the length of the long bar. They face the opposite wall, which is lined with mirrors. To play successfully in this room, a drummer has to keep his wits about him at all times, be utterly fearless, and have the strength of ten to hold the band together. Somehow Jake manages to do all this and still look calm and collected.

"I have to look in the mirror to see who is taking a solo," he said with a grin. "And then I have to look and see what I'm doing."

"He steers us, all sixteen of us," said Phil Wilson, trombonist with the band. "It's like a thing I don't believe is happening."

1963

POSTSCRIPT

Although forty years have gone by, Jake Hanna still maintains his high level of playing and his integrity as a jazz musician. Somehow, throughout his career he resisted becoming a leader, preferring to be the hard-swinging back-up for musicians such as Warren Vaché, Ruby Braff, and Scott Hamilton. Jake and I played many gigs and several recording dates together for the Concord label, and it has always been a kick to work with him. He took time out to get married in the mid-1980s (after years of vowing that he never would) and now lives with his wife, Denisa, in California.

Jake has moved away from the big-band field to a great extent, although he still plays jazz festivals occasionally. Years ago he was with the *Merv Griffin Show* band, but now he concentrates more on small group playing, preferring the easy give-and-take of trios, quartets, and quintets to the less flexible makeup of a big band.

Jake hasn't changed a bit after all these years. His zeal for playing is still as strong as ever, and his enthusiasm, along with his undeniable talent, makes him welcome wherever jazz holds sway.

When I spoke with Jake recently, he told me about various trips he had made to Japan and to festivals in Europe. He is also on the "jazz party" circuit; these parties seem to be proliferating, and now they have even started in England. Although Jake is often involved in them, his mainstay is still small-group playing, which he seems to enjoy more than ever.

He and I enjoyed discussing some of the gigs we played years ago. On one occasion we drove all the way from New York to Florida, except that I did all the driving because Jake said he didn't drive. When we got to Palm Beach I secretly enrolled him in a driving school, so he was quite surprised when the driver showed up with the car for his first lesson. He took the whole course and passed with flying colors, but I later came to suspect that he really *did* know how to drive and went along with the driving school just to keep me happy. I only know that *I* paid for it!

Jake and his wife seem very content in California. Unfortunately, he seldom comes to New York, so I don't get to see him very often. If I did, I know we would soon get involved in telling stories about people we knew years ago, records we made, and anecdotes about the many bands that he has worked with. He has a caustic sense of humor and insisted on calling my husband, Jimmy, "Major Hoople," a cartoon character from the 1950s. I myself have occasionally been the victim of a good-natured Jake Hanna put-down.

To sum it up, Jake really hasn't changed much from the time I met him in the early 1950s. He is playing as well as he ever did—maybe better—and he is still the same good-humored guy, always full of jokes and anecdotes. It's time we got together for a gig.

Benny Goodman: From the Inside— the Sideman's View

About twenty-seven years have gone by since they danced in the aisles to the music of Benny Goodman and his band at the Paramount Theater in New York City. In April 1937 *The New Yorker* ran a profile on "one Benny Goodman." The writer commented in wonderment on "the roar of handclapping, whistling, stamping, and ardent hallooing" that greeted the band at the Paramount. This reception was undoubtedly one of the first of many high points in Benny's career and the one that finally and irrevocably established the great reputation he still retains.

Last November I played with Benny at New York's Philharmonic Hall, and the reception he received from the packed house was not too different from the furor at the Paramount all those years ago. A shade more sedate, certainly . . . no dancing in the aisles . . . but he received a standing ovation, shouts of "bravo," and a sustained roar of applause and whistles that must have gladdened his heart. Quite possibly there were many

Benny Goodman. (George T. Simon Collection)

in the audience that night who had been among the stamping, shouting youngsters who helped cheer him at the Paramount.

Nostalgia was in the air, and the majority of the audience was, as George Avakian said, "a gleamingly pink, paunchy crowd." If Benny ever doubted he could still captivate an audience in the old way, that night, and the many that followed on our subsequent cross-country tour, should have dispelled any doubt.

Benny Goodman is still a great name—a legend—and when he puts a band together and goes out on a concert tour, as he does two or three times a year, he evokes much of the same enthusiasm that he has been generating for the last thirty years. It is, however, to great extent, a nostalgic feeling that pervades the atmosphere. It's nostalgia mixed with admiration that the then-skinny, dark-haired young man with glasses— now a trim fifty-five and as much a master of his instrument as ever—

generates. There are still flashes of sheer inspiration, and the tone, the technique, the masterly, flawless, flowing style is unchanged. Benny represents an era, a way of life, and many who come to hear him relive youth for a brief spell as they listen to the familiar mellow sound of his clarinet, the well-known arrangements with hardly a note changed.

That hardly a note *is* changed is one cause of complaint among some of the musicians who have worked with him in recent years. Tempers flare when new arrangements are discarded in favor of the tried and true—and, to some, outdated—numbers. To these men, the Goodman legend is more a "mystique," a sort of what-makes-Benny-run, that is a never-ending source of discussion, which is always carried on with the enthusiasm one reserves for a subject that never lacks interest or curiosity.

Every time Benny takes out a band there's a fresh flood of stories and anecdotes—some humorous, some tinged with bitterness and anger, many that are probably exaggerated, but all with the unmistakable stamp of this paradoxical man who has confounded, infuriated, snubbed, irritated, thrilled, excited, amused, angered, and enchanted more people than one can shake a (licorice) stick at.

Now that I am an ex-Benny Goodman sideman (or rather sidewoman), I see that it is like being in some special order or fraternity, an in-group. We smile at each other with understanding; we listen avidly to each other's stories of Benny's funny little ways; we compare notes; and those of us to whom he may have been unusually caustic, inconsiderate, or thoughtless can release any left-over resentment in laughter—or sympathy for someone else's experiences. Quite often, though certainly not always, there's an undercurrent of affection and admiration for him running through these stories, but it is mixed with the unholy glee that some musicians obviously feel when recalling and relating their adventures on the road with him.

There seems to be a general air of incredulity regarding B.G. Why does he do the things he does? And what exactly *does* he do or say that makes some musicians want to hurl their instruments to the floor and stomp out furiously? In a way it's like Chinese water torture—it doesn't hurt but it drives you crazy! Benny is as many-faceted as a ten-carat diamond, and to some he appears as cold and hard.

It has been said that at times he doesn't show respect for the musicians who work for him, that he treats them like high-schoolers.

Teddy Wilson, who has played with Benny on and off for thirty years, sums it up: "He doesn't know how to explain what he wants. He acts dissatisfied, yet can't put into words what he'd like to hear. He just knows that whatever they *are* doing—he *doesn't* want that."

What does Benny really want in a musician? It's difficult to know because he never says directly. His suggestions are rather oblique. He'll make an indirect reference to a chord change, emphasize a certain phrasing, give a quizzical look, show sudden amusement at something you don't feel is funny. (I found his famous "ray" to be a sort of stony stare.) These, though seemingly unimportant, are, I believe, some of the things that unnerve those who play with him.

Why has Benny used this approach when a more relaxed attitude would get so much more from his musicians? The average musician is eager to play his best, and given this opportunity and a comfortable climate in which to flourish and grow he'll produce the best music of which he is capable. But in the rarefied atmosphere of a Goodman rehearsal, so often charged with tension, it's enough to make the strongest ego wither from want of nourishment. Or else you rebel! I wonder if Benny realizes just how much these things are discussed, and, if he does, whether he considers them important.

His general attitude to my queries was one of polite tolerance. He was rather guarded, evincing a sort of quiet, off-handed amusement that I should concern myself with such things. I felt that he considered any discussion of the music business—with me at any rate—something to be avoided at all costs. But he stated definitely that he considers any discussion of his fellow musicians somewhat unethical. (Come to think of it, I never have heard him really put down anyone behind his back, except in the mildest possible way.) Not all his fellow musicians share this reticence, however.

"In 1935, I was in the front row at the Texas Centennial to hear the band," Jimmy Giuffre said. "Harry James was in it, Teddy Wilson and Lionel Hampton. I was in high school at the time, and this occasion was one of the most important influences in starting me on my musical career. At that time I could do nothing but admire Benny's playing—the great drive and projection, the fluidity, strong technical fluency, and feeling. He's had more influence on more musicians than anyone else that I can think of. Practically all clarinetists have fallen in behind him. They followed his lead, and it was a good lead.

"He's tried to open up his recent groups to new trends but usually winds up by going back to his old way of doing things. I wrote an arrangement for him once when he had that bop band with Buddy Greco. It was called 'Pretty Butterfly,' but he never used it. Why didn't he use it? Well, if you applied the word 'why' to Benny Goodman you would be in trouble. He throws curves regularly to most people. As an older musician, I think he fears a new era in music that is leaving him behind, so he tries it all for size, and if it doesn't happen to fit he discards it and goes back to his old familiar style. What he's doing now isn't really interesting to *me* anymore because it's the same approach he's used for thirty years. Now it's the expected; *then* it was an innovation. That band he had in 1935 hasn't ever been topped—Benny really knows how to make a band swing—he had good guys, but it was his know-how that made the thing so great.

"But I can't really blame Benny for not going any other route; he picks up the horn, and that's the way he plays. Now, his playing of symphony music . . . the way it sounds is that instead of playing the music on a *personal* basis, he tries to be a legitimate clarinet player with a legitimate sound rather than being Benny Goodman. I feel that he assumes the classical player's role, whereas he should still be *himself* because if anyone has an identity, Benny Goodman has. I feel that jazz music has an identity which is difficult to define; it's a dialect in the player, an accent. I don't know if Benny is trying to prove something to himself by playing classical music in this legitimate style, but, to me, it just doesn't come off. I don't mean that it's bad playing—he's just not in his element, not himself."

Benny's long-time friend and great admirer, composer Morton Gould, takes a somewhat different viewpoint:

> It's impossible to be objective about somebody you feel so strongly about. We would be less than human if we were machinelike in our appraisal. I think that Benny is a first-rate artist; I also feel that too often he is just taken for granted. To me, he has the qualities of a truly great artist—consistent musical integrity. He is very demanding of others, and of himself, and though at times he may be seemingly critical of another person, in my close, intimate contact with him, I have never heard him say anything derogatory, mean, or vicious about another person. He is violently super-critical of *himself.* Perhaps this is why he finds it so hard to find the right people to work with him.
>
> Benny, with all his worldwide success and acclaim, is actually a very shy person. He wants to be left alone. Basically, he's a simple man, with no ostentation—very honest. He has none of the superficial ornamentation that sometimes goes with the public image of a famous personality. He always has his feet on the ground. The legend is that he is unapproachable. Well, basically he *is* an introspective person, and, to me, it's symbolic that a man who has lived through and been a part of as much jazz history as he has could have come away unscathed by the more lurid aspects of the business.
>
> To sum up my feelings about Benny the man, I feel that he is a very warm and compassionate human being, and I have a tremendous admiration for him. There still is a kind of vitality, virtuosity, and imagination in his music. Maybe he's not in vogue just now with the young set, but, nevertheless, his facility and command of the instrument are just as great as they ever were. All you have to do is listen to other clarinetists—and I mean *beyond* jazz—I mean that as a *clarinetist,* not as a jazz artist, he is a fabulous performer. I've heard him play and do things on the highest level of musical art.
>
> Why should a man like Benny Goodman be expected to become far out or be whatever is currently fashionable? All these developments in music are exciting. Popular music, by its very nature, has to change, but somehow one doesn't expect an Elman or a Heifetz

to change his style. I think it's a little unfair to expect one generation to continually remake itself in the image of the generation that
comes after it. It's not in the cards.

Pianist John Bunch, who was with Benny on the 1962 State Department tour of Russia and who also was in the group with which I played,
seems to have insight into some of Benny's other aspects:

> Benny always seems happier with a small group, but really he's
> the most complicated person I've ever met, as far as trying to explain
> him to anyone or to myself. I'm sort of proud that I've been able to
> get along with him so well, personally and musically. I have played
> seven tours with him. The first one was in 1957, and the more I think
> about it . . . wow! . . . the more I wonder how I've managed to stay
> on such good terms with him.
>
> When we were on that Russian thing, Benny played some of my
> arrangements, and I wrote a couple of tunes which he played and
> recorded. . . . A lot of people who haven't had any experience of how
> he acts get pretty shook up, but I was not so disappointed—hell, I
> expected it! Knowing him, I know it doesn't take much to set him
> off, and he really was under a lot of pressure in Russia.
>
> But it's amazing how he seems to have changed since then. He's
> more relaxed, remembers everybody's name, and is generally easier
> to get along with. I don't agree with a lot of the people who put him
> down. When he's really playing—forget about it, he'll scare you to
> death! There's a good reason for his staying on top all these years. It's
> because he can play his head off, and he's had great bands.
>
> Anybody his age with his endurance is really incredible. He'll re-
> hearse for hours, and *we'll* all be getting tired, but he'll just be ready
> to play! One night he came down to The Half Note and sat in with Al
> Cohn and Zoot Sims, and he cooked everybody right off the stand. He
> must have taken ten or fifteen choruses on every tune. We're all a bit
> younger than he is, but we were exhausted when he got through, and
> there he was, fresh as a daisy and ready to play some more!
>
> Anybody that says he can't play—well, they just aren't around
> when he *is* playing. He practices two or three hours a day, and when
> we were rehearsing [for last fall's tour, which was half jazz and half
> classical], he would play for three hours with the Berkshire String

Quartet first—and then start in on the jazz group and rehearse for about five hours straight. He's like a young kid with all that enthusiasm. It just never occurs to him to take a break, because he never gets tired. Most people practice because they have to, but he practices because he loves it.

What's he really like? Well, I've been around a lot of characters in my life, and I can usually predict what all of them will say and do, but you can't predict what *this* guy will do from one minute to the next. When we were out with a group that had Jack Sheldon, Johnnie Markham, and Flip Phillips, Benny was in a real jovial mood the whole time. He was telling jokes. Man, he was a riot. He's got a brilliant mind for comedy, but not too many people know it.

I feel I'm pretty qualified—more than most—to say I know him. A lot of guys have just one brush with him, and they base everything, their opinion of him, on that one experience, which isn't really fair.

"I think a guy that can play as well as he does is entitled to a few eccentricities," said Bobby Hackett, who was in the Lincoln Center group. "I've always found him to be most honorable all around. The trouble with him is that he just can't get his mind off the clarinet. He's like an absent-minded professor, mentally rehearsing all the time. That's why he comes up with these strange remarks sometimes.

"I've worked quite a few weeks with him at different times, and they've all been beautiful. I think a lot of guys that criticize him subconsciously envy his success and his musicianship. Who do you know that pays the kind of salaries he pays? People just don't pay that kind of money, no matter how much they have in the bank. He pays more than anybody and winds up getting criticized. It's like when this country lends money to another country, you make an enemy. Tony Parenti told me a marvelous story once about Benny. In 1930 Tony subbed one night for him in Ben Pollack's band, and instead of cash Benny gave him a baritone sax! That wasn't bad pay for one night."

As marvelous a musician as Benny is, I did notice, however, his seeming lack of interest in rich harmonies. His music reflects this; he always has concentrated on the beat, rhythmic excitement, the melodic line.

Lush voicings and chord changes evidently leave him cold. He seems to want the blandest possible changes behind him, and his improvisations are carried out strictly within this framework. It bothers him to hear an unfamiliar voicing—as I found out. This is his style, however, and his taste; I respect it as such.

As regards his expecting perfection, I can understand this better now, because sometimes I've found that with my own group I will lose patience with a drummer or bass player for not playing the way I think he should play, yet I haven't really told him what I wanted to hear—I just expected him to know.

I think sometimes Benny will hire a musician and expect a great deal from him; then when he finds that he and this person don't have the rapport he thought they would have, he sort of gives up and shuts himself off (I'm second-guessing, as he's never actually told me this). I get the feeling that he expects a musician to know certain intangible things, and if he doesn't catch on at once, then Benny mentally cancels him out.

As a teenager Benny worked harder and more consistently than most people. In fact, he has all his life, and I think he tends perhaps to have a lack of tolerance for people who don't have as great a capacity for work and study as he has, which is understandable. I feel putting down Benny has become a national pastime, and I wonder if the contemporary jazz stars will endure half as long musically, or as people, as he has. I think that at times one tends to grow too emotional about his behavior and that it might be a good idea to examine oneself occasionally instead of always getting mad at Benny.

In retrospect, working for him was a great experience, one from which I have derived a good deal of insight into my own playing and into working with, and playing with, others. Regardless of what people say in favor of, or against, Benny Goodman, his music has endured and will endure. To quote one of Benny's favorite expressions, "the old pepper" is still there.

1964

POSTSCRIPT

I had just gone over these remarks about Benny Goodman when I heard the tragic news that he had died. A feeling of deep sadness came over me for the loss of a friend, the loss of a great musician literally unique in the jazz world, and the end of an era of big-band jazz. Benny was an institution that had always been there. We thought that he would never die. The fact that he was once more leading a band, looking fit, sounding like his old self, heightened this belief. The tragedy is that in the months before his death Benny had found a new lease on life. He had formed a new band, and he was doing just what he wanted to do—playing the clarinet.

On hearing of his death someone said, "Now the Benny Goodman stories will stop." I rather thought they would keep going! Benny, at seventy-seven, was still continuing to amaze, confound, and mystify his followers, who related old and new anecdotes about his eccentricities. Most stories about Benny are funny, but some are strange, and they reveal a Benny no one could ever get to know. Why did he do the odd things he did? Perhaps no one will ever know. One of the stories many people tell about Benny is that during a rehearsal in the garage of his Connecticut home, a musician said, "Benny, it's getting very cold in here." Benny replied, "Oh, yes, it is, isn't it?" And he went into the house and came back with a sweater on! This reminds me of one of the rehearsals I had with Benny at his house. At one point he walked out of the room, so I played a couple of tunes as I waited for him to come back. It seemed that hours went by and there was still no sign of Benny, so I started looking for him. Lo and behold, there he was, in one of the other rooms, trying to choose a reed from several on the table. He saw me standing there and said, "Oh, are you still here?" That's when I knew the rehearsal was over.

It wasn't until later in the tour that I began to get the idea that Benny wasn't too thrilled with my playing. I remember at one point being at a party given for the band, and, after a drink or two, I plucked up enough courage to say to Benny, "Benny, I know you're not happy with my playing—why did you hire me?" Benny gave me a blank stare and mumbled, "I'm damned if I know." Later on, at my suggestion, Benny hired John Bunch to play during Benny's part of the show while I still did my numbers with the trio. However, the night John arrived to take my place, Benny said to him, "Oh, let Marian play the whole show. You can start tomorrow." So I played the show, but at the end Benny asked John Bunch, who was watching from the wings, to come out and play a duet with me. That was a surprise, but John and I loved playing together, and we had a great time playing four hands. At the end of the tune we got a standing ovation; the people wouldn't let us go. Needless to say, Benny never asked us to do that again.

Stories like these are forever a part of the Goodman mystique—and a part of jazz history.

Benny was undoubtedly a genius, and the time (the 1930s) was right for his music to capture the fancy of the entire world. His death brought an end to a whole era of jazz—the Swing Era. That historic time can never return, but this tuneful, rhythmic, lighthearted, and airy music is still being played.

Benny would probably be pleased at the resurgence of this music. People are "swing dancing" once more to what are basically Benny Goodman, the Dorsey Brothers, Artie Shaw, and Glenn Miller tunes, which are being marketed as something new and different. No matter what they call it or how people dance to it, it is still that wonderful swinging music with the insistent beat that brought millions of listeners to jazz years ago. Of course, now people probably wouldn't call it jazz, but to those of us who knew Benny's music (especially to me, having worked with him), it is heartwarming to hear it played once again with the same exciting spirit and verve that it had years ago. Somehow, willy-nilly, we are teaching younger people to enjoy swing music, which they can dance to much more easily than to the sounds of rap and the mindless pop music of today. Long may the memory of Benny Goodman help to keep the swinging sounds and swing dancing part of our culture.

My last meeting with Benny was at Eddie Condon's Club at a party given for George Simon. Benny was in tip-top condition, tanned, trim, smiling—in good spirits. Sad though his passing may be, Benny had a great life. He was considered by many to be the greatest jazz clarinetist who ever lived, he played all over the world, he was adored by his fans and admired by his peers. Indirectly he touched everyone with his music. It was sophisticated yet down to earth. Society people loved it, yet the man in the street could relate to it. Benny as a person was an enigma, but his music was magical and it always will be.

9   Bill Evans, Genius

Bill Evans was the first person I met when I arrived in London for a few weeks' holiday. As I was checking into the hotel he was at the reservations desk making arrangements to stay on for an extra week. It is always a pleasure to see Bill. We don't get a chance to meet very often, and when we do it is usually for a hurried chat between sets at the Village Vanguard or on the phone or at some airport.

This time, at the end of his run at Ronnie Scott's, he was staying in London to relax. After our meeting at the desk, we didn't see each other again for a few days, though we exchanged notes and phone calls as I tried to set up this interview with him for *The Melody Maker*.

We finally arranged to get together, but on the day we were to meet I received a call from Bill. "I'm afraid I can't make it after all, Marian," he said, "but I've written out a couple of things for you, and I'm sending them up."

Shortly after, the bellman brought a carefully notated manuscript

Bill Evans and Marian McPartland during a taping of *Marian McPartland's Piano Jazz*, 1978.

copy of Bill's song "Waltz for Debby" and one of "Very Early," which I thought was a wonderful gift and a graceful gesture showing how considerate a person Bill is.

This sensitive quality comes out in his playing; to me it is the music of a very romantic person—tender, caressing, gentle yet at times strong and vibrant. Bill seems to be a gentle person, though I'm sure this is only one of the many facets of his complex personality that often reveal themselves in his music.

I hear in his playing a level of emotion that doesn't come through in ordinary conversation. Bill speaks in a rather dry monotone. He is very direct and straightforward, with a lively sense of humor that comes out in wry anecdotes and stories about different clubs he has played.

Everything he says is straight to the point. When he warms to a subject, words come pouring out as if he has a great deal to say and very little time in which to say it.

To me, Bill Evans has a special aura, a mystique, an unknown dimension that makes musicians and laymen alike become involved in his music. Is he, indeed, as some say, a genius? Or is he, as Cecil Taylor once said, "merely a cocktail pianist"?

There is little doubt that he is one of the most oft-discussed musicians on the scene today and one of the most widely imitated.

I find his group very interesting to watch as well as listen to, for though they don't indulge in any of the more obvious forms of showmanship (they don't smile or move around), their seriousness is in itself a more natural showmanship, which is real and affecting. All the emotion is in the music, and the intent listener can identify with it.

Bill is immensely tolerant of the musicians in his group, letting them express themselves in the music as they see fit. He once told me: "When a man starts with the trio, I tell him what I want. From then on it is his responsibility to play what is right for each piece. I allow him to come out and contribute in his own way. . . . I want to be involved with my own musical problems, so I expect the others in the group to be attuned to me, and to know instinctively what their role is."

He also appears to be tolerant of the noise element that is such a drawback to working in a nightclub. The only way that he shows he is affected by it is by hunching even closer to the keyboard.

"It's like pulling a blanket around me, shutting everything else out. This way I can concentrate better. But one thing—I never play ballads when the people are noisy."

I finally caught up with Bill. I telephoned him in his room, and he invited me up. He was sitting in an armchair, eating biscuits and drinking milk as if he hadn't had a square meal for days.

"When the job is over I just like to take it easy, not think about appointments or anything," he explained. We talked about the date at Ronnie Scott's and the trio's new drummer, Jack DeJohnette.

"He's very stimulating. He fits in beautifully, filling in in a different way from other drummers. He's a very creative person and plays piano himself, so he has a melodic approach to a song. As a matter of fact, he's getting me off my musical ass."

I said I'd heard that DeJohnette was in effect *forcing* Bill into a more aggressive way of playing.

"People have a certain image of my playing," Evans replied. "They never think of me as a 'hard swinger,' more as a ballad interpreter. Yet they only have to listen to some of my earlier records to realize I have a stronger side to my playing.

"When Philly Joe [Jones] was with the group he got me into playing harder." (Philly has been quoted as saying: "Playing with Bill is one of the most beautiful things that could happen to a drummer.")

We talked about Bill Evans's early influences: "Well, Nat Cole was one of my major ones . . . Earl Hines, a lot of horn players, people you never heard of, I listen to everybody here and there. But my main influence, if you really want to know, was Bud Powell."

I wondered whether there were any recordings of Bill and bassist Scott LaFaro still unreleased. "Just one of the things we made the night before he died. Everything we played has been put out except 'I Love You, Porgy.'"

How about new material for the trio?

> Once in a while I pull a set out of the hat—new things we've never played before—but not of course when I'm under rigid set conditions like a Saturday night at the Vanguard.
>
> We never rehearse really, so everything is out of the hat one way or another. But I have to have a basic repertoire because we must pace our sets and we don't play long tunes, so naturally we fall into a lot of the same things.
>
> But I want some new tunes . . . we're doing a couple now—"Mother of Pearl" and Eddie [Gomez] does "Embraceable You" as a feature; and we're doing Denny Zeitlin's "Quiet Now."

Evans started to get more animated, talking and drinking more milk as he expressed his thoughts.

> You know, Marian, when I was in the band at home in my teens I used to come right out and say things to the other musicians, and I'd move right up front and take over—not just to take over but perhaps because I could see nobody else could handle it.
>
> This is when I was about fourteen. But I always knew the reason for everything I did, and when I play I know exactly what I'm doing. Years ago I had dreams about composing. I was really set on jazz in a very deep way, but I feel my childhood was squashed, musically speaking, because nothing was done about it.
>
> Later, I learned basic things, like counterpoint and music analysis. Kids should get all this at eleven or twelve, but in America they're just taught to read music, they don't get any theory.
>
> My advice to kids is to learn how music is put together and to start as early as they're interested. A child enjoys solving problems.

I asked what his advice would be to young piano players starting out. He said:

> I'd say: Know clearly what you're doing. Play much less and be very clear about it. How far can you go on instinct? Then it gets to be just rhapsodic confusion.
>
> The thing you are going to build on must be basic. As you learn

how music is put together you will know how to create. It's much better to spend thirty hours on one tune than to play thirty tunes in one hour.

Listening to Bill talk, I thought about what his friend Pat Smythe said about him: "He imposes his own aura on every tune he plays, and he has, above all, the ability to give a performance which can only be described as magical. This magic conveys itself to musicians and nonmusicians alike." To put it in my own way, Bill is one of a kind as a pianist, composer, and as a human being.

1968

POSTSCRIPT

Every pianist in the jazz world (and many in the classical world) admires Bill Evans. His untimely death in 1980 only seemed to make his music more deeply felt. His records sell better than ever. More than a legend, more than a cult figure, Bill seems almost Messianic in his influence, and his music has become an integral part of jazz history.

My friendship with Bill dated back to 1953, when I first heard him at the Village Vanguard with Scott LaFaro and Paul Motian, and we often performed at the same festivals and concerts.

So much happened in Bill's life after this article was written, including the deaths of his father (for whom he wrote "Turn Out the Stars") and of his wife Elaine. But later, when he remarried and his son, Evan, was born, Bill seemed to play on an even more creative level than before. The events of his life seemed to mesh and to give him greater emotional depth and sensitivity. His writing became increasingly poignant, as can be heard in such songs as "B-Minor Waltz," one of the most beautiful of all his compositions. The wistful melody speaks of untold sorrows.

It is still hard to realize Bill is gone, but his music is heard wherever jazz is played, and his influence is felt even more deeply in the more than twenty years since his death. It seems like yesterday that Bill was my guest on *Piano Jazz* in 1978, the first year of our show, when we were recording at the Baldwin Piano Showroom. I'm amazed and thrilled at how well Bill and I played together, and I still feel very happy that I had this opportunity to learn firsthand what it was like to get an inside glimpse, a feeling of Bill's playing that I would never have got from just listening to him. My interview with Bill on *Piano Jazz* is very precious to me, and when I hear it I relive the many marvelous times that I heard Bill and his trio over the years. The fact that we played together so well still amazes me. Perhaps we meshed so perfectly because, although I have never consciously tried to copy Bill's playing, his harmonic concept and wonderfully executed single lines have never ceased to intrigue me. There is always some new facet to be discovered as one listens.

The years have gone by, and many of today's young musicians are getting turned on to Bill Evans. Admiration for him just keeps on growing, but the mystery of his life is still unfolding. Why did a man with all that talent, who seemed so straight-ahead, so normal and organized, at the same time contribute to his own death in a way that he certainly must have known would shorten his life? Our recording session was such a wonderful experience. How could I know that within a year Bill would have died from the effects of his lifelong heroin addiction? Seeing him there that afternoon, so completely together, full of jokes and good humor, one could never guess that he had returned to his old habit. Of all the occasions that I got together with Bill over the years, that afternoon stays in my memory as one of the most wonderful times two musicians could spend together. When he died I was devastated, but at the same time I was angry with him for doing this to himself and depriving us, his friends and fans, of many more years of exquisite music.

I have so many small reminders of Bill around the house—not only a huge collection of his recordings but also books and personally signed manuscripts, some of which I brought back to him the day we did *Piano Jazz* just to have him update them and sign them a second time, which amused him greatly. I was a true groupie where Bill was concerned.

Despite the growth of avant-garde music and a seeming desire on the part of some musicians to stretch the boundaries as far as they possibly can, Bill Evans's incandescent, melodic playing and his harmonic genius still prevail.

10 Looking to the Future: Ron McClure and Eddie Gomez

Scott LaFaro's name almost automatically springs to mind whenever a new bassist comes on the scene. The memory of LaFaro's playing often serves as the yardstick against which the newcomer is measured. And those who admired him are prone to overlook whatever distinctiveness a new bassist has—the same cry is heard: "He sounds just like Scottie."

In a sense, LaFaro, who died in 1961, lives on in the young players who have consciously or unconsciously come under his influence, briefly or deeply.

Ron McClure and Eddie Gomez are two young bassists who often have been likened to LaFaro. They both have the ill-defined quality called "potential."

Both of them have worked with my trio on and off for the last two or three years. Though at times one or the other would leave to play with other groups, we nevertheless were together a great deal, enabling me

Ron McClure.

Jimmy McPartland, Marian McPartland, and Eddie Gomez, 1969.

to get to know them well, to admire and respect their talents, and to appreciate them as friends. I soon became aware that though they were from entirely different environments, they were alike in aims, goals, and outlook.

McClure, twenty-four, is of Scotch-Irish and German heritage, from a comfortably-off and conservative Connecticut background, the youngest of three brothers.

Eddie Gomez, twenty-one, born in Santurce, Puerto Rico, of a lower-middle-class family, the elder of two sons, was brought to the United States before his first birthday and has lived most of his life in the uptown section of New York City.

Neither comes from a musical family; neither chose the bass of his own volition—yet both pursue the same musical course. Both want to attain perfection, to reach new peaks in the development of their instrument, to be innovators, to give of themselves, and to gain recognition. Both are succeeding in their goals, yet each remains unique. They are talented, possibly even brilliant, musicians. Each is extremely versatile and always aware of the role he plays in a group, seeming to know what is right for any particular musical situation.

Gomez is a less flamboyant player than McClure. Short in stature and serious-looking, he goes about his business quietly. To the casual observer he appears detached, yet at times will surprise the listener with sound effects that seem startling coming from such a studious-looking young man.

With Ron, it is all pent-up emotion. When he plays, he is lost to the world—eyes closed, his involvement with the music complete. He seems at one with his instrument as he plucks, strokes, flays, and strums the strings to ring out a varied assortment of sounds. He has a most unusual technique that at times involves an odd turning of his left hand, the better to achieve the particular idea he wants. He often uses double-stops, triple-stops, and what sound like quadruple-stops. Such is his ability, he apparently can play anything he hears in his head. He is a musician who obviously loves to play.

"I like to get into it," McClure said. "If you're really involved in playing, you don't think about anything else—I don't like to see someone smiling and looking nice, completely detached from the music. I always have to get involved."

Ron's ability on his instrument is expanding all the time as he gains insight from his various musical experiences of the last few years. Since early 1964 he has worked alternately with Maynard Ferguson and with my husband Jimmy and myself, and we have literally watched him grow musically. Though there is a certain similarity to LaFaro in the long lines he plays and in his tender lyricism, the resemblance ends there, for though he acknowledges LaFaro as one of his major influences, Ron is his own man—in technique, touch, time-feeling, and as a soloist.

In the last few months he has changed from a young bassist of promise to a fast-maturing musician of truly enormous talent. On his clearly enunciated solos, his ideas pour out; each chorus is meaningful. He seems to release a part of himself when he plays.

"Red Mitchell is the one who is indirectly responsible for at least half my bass playing," Ron said. "He has always been my heaviest influence on solos. I gobbled up every record he ever made as fast as they came out—listening to him sure warms my heart."

McClure also has admiration for Steve Swallow, whom he describes as "the best young bass player there is. He can do no wrong in my book. His ensemble playing is impeccable; if I could do it half as well, I'd be satisfied."

Swallow, in turn, has expressed his respect and liking for McClure. "He's a very adventurous, athletic, vigorous player," Swallow said, "and he plays in the middle range of the instrument, which is unusual. It is the most difficult area to play in—to make it speak clearly. Most players jump from the high to the low register to circumvent the problem. Also, I have an idea his fiddle is not set up for easy playing; he seems like the kind of musician who doesn't care to make any compromises."

Of Gary Peacock McClure observed, "Gary's beautiful . . . he has gorgeous hands. He can put on those bursts of speed. The man plays with such conviction, there's nothing insipid about him at all. He's got something that's really his own."

In his generous assessment of the talents of others, McClure is apt to be modest about his own accomplishments. He is quite a good pianist and likes nothing better than to be left alone at the piano, experimenting with different chord changes, playing fragments of the beautiful tunes he improvises. He has managed to get a few of these down on paper, and one of them, currently titled "Nimbus," is a tour de force every time he plays it.

McClure appears to be universally liked, not only for his talent but also for his happy-go-lucky way. He is a mixture of raffish humor with a touch of shyness and brashness, even saltiness, which mask his sensitivity. Most important of all is his eagerness to play at the drop of a hat. These qualities and his great endurance—gained during his many months with Ferguson's big band—make him one of today's most sought-after musicians.

McClure's home is in North Haven, Connecticut. His two brothers were so much older that as a child he hardly knew them and grew up in a world of his own. When he was five, he asked his mother for an accordion.

"It was really my idea," he said, "and I wanted to take lessons. So my mother got me a small accordion, and I started studying with a local guy."

As he became more proficient on the accordion, Ron changed to a full-sized instrument and assembled a group that played at local functions. He started playing in the school band as well.

"We'd play 'stocks,' you know—'Linger Awhile,' and things like that," he said, "then I started playing bass drum in the marching band too. At the time, they asked me if I wanted to play bass or the marching drum, and I chose the drum."

He later was persuaded to switch from accordion to bass, and he started studying privately with a well-known Hartford, Connecticut, teacher, Joe Iadone. At fifteen Ron was beginning to get thoroughly immersed in music.

When he was graduated from high school, his one idea was to go to college and study music full time, but his parents did their best to dissuade him, pointing out the dissolute life they thought he would face as a jazz musician. To please them he enrolled in a business school in Hartford, but, as his mother said, "the bass went with him." After one semester both Ron and his parents knew that this was no good, and he insisted they allow him to enroll at the Julius Hart College of Music in Hartford. Having won their approval, he registered the next day and embarked on a full-time course of study, continuing his private lessons with Iadone, who instilled in him a solid musical background. McClure speaks of Iadone with respect and affection, and it is evident that the teacher is largely responsible for bringing out McClure's talent.

"I could see he was exceptional from the very beginning," Iadone said, "and as far as his jazz playing is concerned, I recognized this in him immediately, and I always knew that he would do well."

McClure started playing at the Heublein Hotel in Hartford with pianist Dave Mackay, who, with drummer Joe Porcaro ("the finest musician I've ever met," McClure said), helped him gain valuable experience as a jazz player. During this time McClure also rehearsed with different groups, sat in wherever he could, played some dates at McTriff's Bar in New Haven, and listened to as much music as possible.

There was some disapproval at the school at such goings-on, especially since an occasional rehearsal or lesson would be cut in order to make a jazz gig. But in this carefree fashion McClure managed to absorb a great deal of music.

A pianist friend, Meryl Doucette, broadened Ron's musical scope considerably by playing records for him hour after hour, and it was in this way that he learned to appreciate the long, fluid bass lines played by Paul Chambers as he and Doucette listened to Miles Davis and Red Garland records.

"That's the way I've always wanted to play," Ron said. "I've always dug the way Paul played time—it's so loose. There was one particular record, *Four* by Miles, that I liked a lot. The sound that Paul gets is what I always strive for and have tried to get in my own playing."

In 1962 McClure graduated from the Julius Hart School. After giving a successful classical recital, at which he was accompanied by Doucette, he left—without even waiting to receive his diploma—for a date in Chicago with Porcaro, vibist Mike Mainieri, and pianist Bruce Martin, later flying to Las Vegas with Mainieri for his first important engagement, with Buddy Rich's small band. After a few months the group broke up, and McClure went back east to start a long series of engagements with the Ferguson band. In between were dates with Don Friedman and a six-month stint with Herbie Mann, which the bassist, ambitious and bursting with creativity, found a little too restrictive (he still chafes at any sort of regimentation).

It was shortly after Ron left Mann's group last year that Eddie Gomez (who was leaving my trio for West Coast engagements with Gary McFarland) recommended him to me, speaking warmly of his ability. All last year Maynard Ferguson and I shared the talents of McClure. (And it was lucky for me that during the times Ron was with Maynard, Gomez was available and worked with me. I would go about smugly, saying, "Happiness is having two great bass players!")

We continued pretty much in this manner until a few weeks ago: Gomez flew down to Florida to work with Jimmy and me at Christmas, and he played all of January at Les Champs with Jake Hanna and me. Ron went with us to Fort Lauderdale in February and March, then rejoined Maynard for several weekends at the Village Gate. During this period the Ferguson group worked opposite guitarist Wes Montgomery, who was impressed with Ron's playing, and invited him to take Paul Chambers's place with his accompanying group. The idea of replacing one of his idols was and is still overwhelming to Ron, and the fact that he is playing with another of his longtime favorites, pianist Wynton Kelly, is for him almost unbelievable.

Montgomery is euphoric about McClure's playing, saying, "He's beautiful—superb—his playing fits this group like a glove."

To McClure, rehearsing every day, learning new music, working with top-flight musicians he admires and respects, and being in a musical situation he can grow in and thrive on is one of his many dreams coming true.

The fulfillment of a dream that he never quite dared believe might actually happen came true for Eddie Gomez when pianist Bill Evans asked him to join his trio last month. For Gomez, this is the culmination of all his hopes and his striving for perfection.

"I'm ecstatic; I can hardly believe it," he said.

Ironically, if it had not been for the sharp eyes of one of his grade school teachers Gomez might not have been a bassist.

"I wanted the cello—anything but the bass," Gomez recalled, "but I hadn't played an instrument at all till that time. [He was eleven.] I used to sing in the choir—I was always a ham in class—but then one day the teacher looked at my fingers and told me I was going to play the bass. It was a half-size bass, naturally. I had no individual involvement with the instrument, but I did have a deep burning desire to play music; so when I got the bass I really dove into it. I wanted to be a good craftsman, and I rehearsed a lot. And soon I started hounding my father for lessons and a bass of my own, but I didn't get either of them until I was in high school."

At this time, the thirteen-year-old Gomez started taking lessons from Fred Zimmerman, the famous New York City teacher. Gomez had heard of Marshall Brown's Newport Youth Band and was determined to play with it. When he found out that Brown was auditioning musicians, he applied.

"I was just getting through for the day when there came a knock on the door," Brown recalled. "I opened it, and there was this small kid standing there—he was unbelievably small. 'I'd like to audition for the band,' he said. Well, I was pretty spoiled—I'd had Andy Marsala and guys like that, and I said no, I didn't think he could do it. Man, he was no bigger than the main part of the bass; he was just too goddamn small!

"But he insisted that he be heard, so I took him inside. One of the kids was playing the bass, and, as we listened, I said to Eddie, 'Do you really think you're ready?' and he said, 'Yeah!' So I said, 'Can you play like that fellow?' and he said, 'Yeah, sure!' And he took the bass and played ten times better! He was totally confident. He used rather unorthodox fingering, but who cared. He was swinging already, and his time was *great!*

"I took him on as an alternate bass player, and then he became the regular bass player six months later. He was the youngest kid to ever join the union, and when we went out on the road playing these ballrooms, it was really illegal for him to be on the stage, but I'd sneak him on to play one number. Then later when he joined the band on a steady basis we'd do a lot of weekends—Hershey Park, Pennsylvania, places like that—all the other kids would be roistering about and carrying on in the back of the bus and in the middle of all this chaos was Eddie, reading and smoking a pipe. He was always a grown-up, never a baby, and I never talked down to him or treated him like a hippy. But I used to kid him about being fifteen going on forty.

"When I broke up the band in 1960, he was then technically one of the better bass players in town, and he was only sixteen. The only thing was, nobody knew it except me, but I knew it was just a question of time before Bill Evans found him. He's like another Jimmy Blanton."

In the last three years, since he started working with my trio in the Strollers Club for the *Establishment* show, Eddie has crammed in a great deal of playing and study. When we met, he was going to Juilliard, and he continued his courses there, though he was playing every night until 3:00 A.M. and getting up again at 7:00 A.M. to go to school. The previous year he had got married, and his wife Amy was expecting a baby. (His son was christened Scotty.)

The job at the Strollers ended in November 1963, and shortly after Eddie was offered a string of dates with Gary McFarland. The chance to play with such a fine musician tempted Eddie to leave Juilliard without completing his course of study. The band went to the West Coast and also played at the *Down Beat* Jazz Festival.

Of late, Gomez has been in demand for a variety of groups. He went to Boston for a week with guitarist Jim Hall, of whom Gomez says, "He has a softness—he's such a passionate type of player. He's brought so much music to his instrument." Recently Eddie played several weekends with Gerry Mulligan at the Village Vanguard, and that is where he was heard by Evans, who was working opposite.

"When you hear a guy playing a solo on a melody that you're familiar with," Gomez said, "you can tell if he's playing the changes and playing the correct rhythm just by using the knowledge you've been brought up on. That's why we relate to harmony and basic rhythm, but when you listen to someone like Archie Shepp, you don't have that kind of gauge to go by—it's unlike anything you've learned before. In a way, it's like listening to a poet: does he incite beautiful feelings in you, even if he doesn't make complete sense to you from a conventional standpoint? You have to leave yourself open, to *want* to listen, to want him to give you something. . . . Chances are, you'll get something from it if you have this attitude.

"People go to concerts to hear the avant-garde players with the idea of trying to find out what they are doing, but that's not why they are playing for you. They're trying to give you a musical journey, and you're not supposed to care where it takes you or why. It takes just a little more openness, trying to get with something you don't understand. But to criticize it out of hand is like talking to somebody and prejudging them, judging them on a surface level. So, instead, you say, 'I'll take a few punches from you, and see what's in you,' and it's worthwhile to do that because you find something out about that, and something about yourself too.

"But it's hard to do, because the whole country is geared in the other direction—to take everything at its surface value. Speaking about that, once you reach that mass appeal, you can't be as creative in the same proportion as you were before you reached that level. You have to sacrifice a certain amount of fresh searching and probing to give people what they want to hear—after all, you've got farmers in Minnesota depending on you now."

It is observations like these that make Gomez a stimulating, humorous, and often profound conversationalist as well as musician. He thinks on a very high level and with tolerance, kindness, and a complete absence of malice. He loves to talk about music and musicians.

"A freer, less rigid drumming is really the secret of playing today," he maintains. "The drummer can be open, or he can freeze things up—literally stop production. With some groups, you're right in the middle of the square, where only certain moves will fit. Now, take Tony Williams: as free as he plays, the time is always there somewhere—even if it's only an eighth note. I love his playing."

"I'd like to work in as many different musical environments as possible," Gomez went on to say, "and to be given the chance to express myself within each one. I think all musicians like to feel they have been called for a job because of their creative individuality—like, because you do your thing, and they want you because you're *you*. With Bill Evans it's a mutual exchange. Yet, in a way, it's very demanding: because he lets me play so much, I can see I have a lot of work cut out for myself. There is a very strong musical thing between him and me—a great musical understanding."

"We're going to get along just fine—I'm looking forward to having a long-term development with Eddie," said Evans, sounding unusually excited. "Having him is a tremendous thing for me. He's doing just beautifully, and I'm extremely happy. I think being with the group has done Eddie a lot of good already, and I'm letting everybody know how I feel about him. I'm *really* excited. At this point I don't know what we're going to get into . . . he's just bubbling over, and his ideas come pouring out. He has that same sort of quality that Scott had when I first heard him—he wanted to say so much, he almost played twelve solos at one time. When he reined in was when he really started communicating. I'm looking forward to getting together to play some with Eddie when we get to the West Coast, in the afternoons, quietly, without the strain of performances at night."

Questioning Gomez about his influences elicits intelligent, well-thought-out responses. He is enthusiastic about his favorite players:

"Charlie Mingus was the one at the very beginning of that era of opening the bass up, furthering it along the path to be a more creative voice. Another guy I've always liked, too, is Ray Brown. I dig his sound and choice of notes behind the soloist—he's into the music all the time. Of course, it was Scott LaFaro who really showed clearly what the bass was going to be doing for a long time to come.

"When anybody plays fast, they think it's a style of playing, whereas having good-enough chops to play fast should be part of the equipment. We basically use all the same technical equipment, but it's what a person plays that tells how individual he is. Now, Gary [Peacock] plays punctuated short lines—a singing, ringing kind of sound, like a guitar. There are so many beautiful sounds to be gotten out of the bass. That's what Steve Swallow's got going. He's another guy who has a unique way of doing things. Yet from a solo standpoint I think Red Mitchell was one of the first bass players to have brought people's ears to a bass solo by using a different technique—sort of a flamenco style. . . .

"Among young bass players, I think Cecil McBee and Albert Stinson are two of the most promising. There are not that many bass players—not that many who really care—but I think the kids who are geared for being creative are around. They're the ones who won't bother with rock-and-roll. Bass playing has got to such a high level now that you expect more and want more from them. In fact you demand more! I want to enlarge the scope of the bass—get more sounds, more playing in the upper register, and there are so many wonderful things to do in the lower register too. It's not easy to build a solo, but I like to play solo lines and to do things with other people—and a freer context is more conducive to that. Playing in 4, and making it swing, is hard, but there's more to it than that.

"The young kids should listen not only to bass players but to *all* music—to be more of a *musician* as opposed to being a bass player. Of course, sight reading, technique, etc., are necessary musical equipment, unless you use them as an end instead of a means. Properly used, it's like a rug for you to stand on, so that you have a way of doing something. Lack of it is not a sign of being a creator, but having it doesn't mean that you are a mere craftsman either. However, it's the two combined that make an artist. It's the trend now to have good chops, and you have to have a certain amount of aggressiveness to play.

"There's so much to do—so much happening. At one time I was very much involved with Ray Brown's playing, then I heard Bill and Scottie, and the music that came after that, like Paul Bley—he's such a romantic player—and Ros Rudd. There's a lot of wholesome music there, but I don't want to do just that. I dig 4/4, and I like beautiful chord progressions. There's a lot to be done with this yet and something to be learned about adapting yourself to what the musical point is of the group you're with, what point is being made. If you go off by yourself, you don't have a trio, you just have the other people—and you. But if you listen to what's going on around you, you soon get your ideas of what to do. I call it subtle individualism.

"Now, take the way the time is being played in some of the newer groups today: you're only on the surface level of what *can* be done. Break that surface, and there's a whole lot more underneath. There's no basic rhythm to do it for you—you have to be a world within yourself. You're using your brain, and it involves a lot more regimentation than people think, because the time is not put before your very eyes, as it is in more conventional playing. I guess the way music is today, you have to make your choice: to be a record-date player or a *player*. I want to *play*. I would go anywhere on this earth to play good music."

1965

POSTSCRIPT

In the years since this piece was written I have come to appreciate these two musicians even more for their valuable contributions to jazz and their continuing search for new ways to express themselves musically.

Both men have more than fulfilled their early promise. In 1972 Ron McClure joined the faculty at the Berklee College of Music and a few years later joined Blood, Sweat and Tears, with whom he recorded his composition "Mirror Image" as well as several albums. Later he worked with Jack DeJohnette (as did Eddie Gomez), then spent three years with the Dave Liebman Quartet, traveling and recording. He returned to teaching at Long Island University for a while and performed in workshops and jazz clinics all over the country. In 1985 Ron entered a new phase of his career by joining Quest, a group headed by Richie Beirach, performing with them at a number of concerts and festivals. With many records and compositions to his credit, Ron McClure lives a full and satisfying life, recording and playing the music of his choice, arranging and composing new pieces, and working with students eager to learn every facet of his art.

Eddie Gomez was twenty-one when he joined Bill Evans's group. He was with Bill for eleven years, and some of the group's most memorable albums were made during that time. Eddie continued to impress everyone with his ever-changing, ever-growing approach to the bass. After leaving Bill he (as well as Ron McClure) worked for a while with Jack DeJohnette in New Directions, a co-op band. Later he joined the group Steps Ahead with Michael Brecker and Steve Gadd.

Eddie has been in great demand for recording dates and tours to Europe and the Orient. He has worked with Miles Davis, Chick Corea, McCoy Tyner, Herbie Hancock, and other top groups and has recorded albums under his own name. Eddie has always gone straight ahead and has had further success as the leader of his own group.

It is heartening to know that the potential shown by these two players has developed over the years into a long and impressive list of credits. With their still-evolving talents they continue to look to the future, and it looks good.

❖

In order to find out what Ron and Eddie are doing these days, I contacted each of them and got caught up in all their various activities. It seems that both of them are going forward with their successful careers, each in a different way.

Since Eddie left Bill Evans in 1977, his career has continued in an upward mode with a variety of new projects; he has even ventured into the classical music world by performing with the Tashi Ensemble, Kronos Quartet, and clarinetist Richard Stoltzman. He has also crossed over into the pop world, performing with pop icons Carly Simon, Michael Franks, and Art Garfunkel. Some of the jazz people he has worked with, such as Chick Corea, have won Grammy Awards, but Eddie himself is still looking forward to winning a Grammy for his own group. He has always been a musician who is deeply involved in all aspects of music—composing, playing, educating, and arranging. I recently learned that he was getting ready for a tour of Japan with his group as well as becoming involved in projects for film.

A short time ago I had Eddie as a guest on *Piano Jazz* and was reminded again what a marvelous player he is and how compatible we are when playing together. On the show we talked about dates we had played before he started working with Bill Evans, and in retrospect some of those dates were great fun. Working at the Strollers Club in New York was probably the only time Eddie had a speaking part in a play—*The Establishment,* the British comedy show that was performed onstage before we started playing in the Back Room. At one point in the play the folks onstage watched a film of Queen Elizabeth and Prince Philip riding through London in a gilded coach. John Bird (onstage) would say, "She's every inch a queen!" Offstage, Eddie would say into the microphone, "And so is he!" Often those of us backstage would try to make Eddie miss his cue, which was typical of the juvenile pranks that were continuously going on. After all these years we still reminisce about some of the funny stuff that went on in this club in the early 1960s.

Eddie is a little more serious now; his son Scotty is thirty-seven years old and has two children of his own. It's hard to believe that the eighteen-year-old bass player who started working with me in the 1960s is a grandfather! I'm sure there are many more ways in which Eddie Gomez will be fulfilling his creative life with new projects and musical activities planned for the future—new compositions, recording dates, and work with his many friends, such as Michael Brecker, will keep him busy and active for a very long time to come.

Although it had been a while since I last spoke with Ron McClure, I had seen his name in many jazz magazines and on records. He has at least fifteen CDs to his credit on Steeplechase as leader and composer of the music. When we spoke recently, I learned of his many engagements in various parts of the world. He has been to Buenos Aires, Finland, Sweden, Austria, and Germany, giving master classes and lectures.

He also has several CDs on the Naxos label, and on listening to the newest one, *Double Triangle,* I realized that Ron has lost none of his creative ideas as both a composer and bassist. Some of his solos are quite remarkable in their ingenuity—filled with musical ideas born of his years of playing with so many top-flight musicians. Being the bass player, producer, and leader of his own group seems to have spurred him on to create some memorable lines and structures conducive to improvisation and creative interplay among all the musicians in the group. He told me of a forthcoming tour to Argentina with Lee Konitz, and recently I was able to catch him at a New York club with pianist and composer Phil Markowitz. Ron has always been a tremendously good reader, and he needs to be in order to play the kind of music that Phil writes. It was interesting to hear how good the group sounded with Ron on bass and Glenn Davis on drums, keeping the time "right in the pocket." It's obvious that Ron continues to be one of the most sought-after bassists on the scene, and with his many recordings, his composing, and piano playing, he is assured of an active and busy musical life for a long time to come. The years have brought him both successes and trials, but as a tried-and-true jazz player he keeps right on swinging!

Dudley Moore: Serious Music from a Colossus of Comedy

Recently, I had the pleasure of getting reacquainted with Dudley Moore, who was a guest on my National Public Radio show. I hadn't seen Dudley for the past fifteen years (except in his various movies and television appearances), so it was a real joy to hear him play solo jazz piano and to join him in some duets. Actually, we *had* played together (four hands, one piano) years ago at the wedding of a mutual friend. I knew then what a fine jazz player Dudley was, and now I have learned how unusual he is in that he plays jazz and the classics equally well.

Dudley had just returned to California from New York, where he appeared in concert at Carnegie Hall, playing the Beethoven Triple Concerto with the St. Paul Chamber Orchestra to a sellout crowd of enthusiastic fans. He subsequently repeated this same program in Los Angeles, getting an equally triumphal reception; he had been well treated by the critics at both concerts and was feeling relaxed and happy.

Dudley Moore and Marian McPartland while taping *Marian McPartland's Piano Jazz*, 1982.

"This is my last gig for four months," Dudley said as he noodled on the piano, making little passes at it, trills, runs, and glisses, as if punctuating every remark. While we played through different tunes for the taping, he told me he had been practicing more than eight hours a day for several months to get ready for the Beethoven concerto. I marvelled that he could do this on top of all his movie and television commitments. "I must be nuts," Dudley grinned and laid down some heavy dissonant chords, ending in a burst of arpeggios up and down the keyboard.

Dudley Moore was born in Dagenham, a suburb east of London. His mother played the piano, so her son grew up to the sounds of music at home. It seemed only natural that he would start playing the piano himself, by ear at first. Then his parents, sensing a special talent, started him with a piano teacher at the age of six. After a while he began studying the violin, harpsichord, and organ (he later won an organ scholarship to prestigious Oxford University).

Dudley's gift for humor had also surfaced. He was cutting up for the kids in school and singing and playing witty parodies of the classics, making the most of his natural musical talent. A voracious reader, he started digging into all kinds of books and making constant trips to the library and the local music store. "I wanted to pick up sheet music all the time," Dudley recalls. "I couldn't wait to try a new piece, because I loved hearing all those little black dots come alive. I couldn't get enough of it! I sang in the church choir, too. The church was opposite our house, so I sort of fell into that naturally. I loved to sing and I still do—I'm a great countertenor! Then, when I was about thirteen, I got friendly with some kids that had a group, and we put a piano on a lorry and rode around town playing for people. I really felt good about doing that."

At age sixteen Dudley was turned on to jazz. He heard a record of Erroll Garner playing "The Way You Look Tonight," which added to his musical life considerably. He was totally fascinated and set about learning to play in the Garner style and collecting all the Gamer records he could find. "I loved that steady beat in the left hand and the way the melody sort of wriggles around inside that rhythm," Dudley remembers. "There used to be a jazz club at the top of our street. It looked a bit like a bordello, and a lot of guys played there. I used to go and sit in. Everybody was listening to [saxophonist] Lee Konitz at the time, but I was so crazy about Garner I just wanted to listen to him, although I was hearing a lot of other pianists, too—Oscar Peterson, Art Tatum, Nat Cole, Stan Kenton."

Dudley had some experiences with big bands. "I was with Vic Lewis in 1959, but everybody in the band got mad at me because I played Garner-style behind the soloists! I didn't know how to back up people in those days." He later played with John Dankworth's group—by then he *had* learned to comp! Just last year he cut an album with Cleo Laine (Mrs. John Dankworth) that illustrates his flexibility as an accompanist [*Smilin' Through,* Finesse Records]. The same sensitivity and intuitiveness I heard on this record came through when we played duets for the radio program taping. Dudley *listens,* and he knows when to back up the other player (he laid down a bristling bass line!) and when to take over.

It's obvious that Dudley is a romantic. He plays ballads with a fervor and passion that he cannot hide. Some of his favorite tunes include "Smilin' Through," "Autumn in New York," "Sweet and Lovely," and Noël Coward's "I'll See You Again." He reveres the English contralto Kathleen Ferrier [1912–53] and has all her records. "There is such passion, beauty, and poetry in her singing," he says. "Every time I listen to her it is a new emotional experience."

Dudley's original compositions (some of which have been featured in his films) have a plaintive, melancholy air, and for our show he combined the "Charlotte" and "Nicole" themes from his movie *Six Weeks,* performing them with a lingering, delicate sound. Dudley has a good command of the keyboard and a firm yet lyrical touch. He seems to favor a middle-of-the-road tempo that is pulsating and buoyant. "That's heartbeat time," Dudley explains; "120 on the metronome. Everything I like to play seems to fit into that little spot." It's interesting to note that, while some areas of his musical mind are shooting off in all directions, he is still just as obsessed with Erroll Garner as he was at sixteen. He started our program with the same piece he first heard on that memorable record, "The Way You Look Tonight," and Erroll would have loved it. Then I asked him to play the same piece in his own style. He seemed surprised, but he put together a beautiful rubato treatment of it. "You can't go wrong with Jerome Kern," Dudley said, and followed with a translucent version of "Long Ago and Far Away."

Dudley Moore appears to be a man of many facets—part humorist, part romantic, part musician, *definitely* part crazy, and part serious, too. Yet you just *know* he's ready to break into some insane singing or bash out wild chords at the drop of a flatted fifth! On some of his improvisations these flashes of humor surface—the imp and the musician merging with impunity.

On ballads one notices his appreciation of the rich voicings of the French Impressionists, but there are strong overtones of liturgical music in his playing, as well as melodic ideas stemming from his knowledge of English folk songs. When I asked about his organ studies at Oxford, he played most of a Handel prelude and fugue without thinking twice about it.

Instead of resting on his laurels and acknowledging the acclaim he's receiving from his recent film hits *Arthur* and *10,* Dudley is planning to take on some more heavy musical tasks with the dedication and drive he gave to the Beethoven Triple Concerto. He has a steadfast desire to play the classical repertoire well, and he seems to have a need to set new goals for himself. In so doing he is commanding a new respect and admiration from musicians everywhere. Though he is an idealist, he believes in hard work—a craftsman of concertos *and* comedy.

With his well-rounded musical background, it seems only natural that Dudley would be drawn into this new musical situation which has given him such deep satisfaction: performing classical music in concert. In 1959 he was appearing at the Edinburgh Festival in the now legendary four-man revue *Beyond the Fringe.* Here he met violinist Robert Mann, leader of the famed Juilliard String Quartet, and he became totally fascinated by their brilliant chamber music. Mutual admiration and a quickly growing friendship sprang up between the two men, which soon led to a series of musical evenings, presided over by Mann, every time Dudley came to New York. He became more and more involved in playing chamber music with Mann and other fine musicians.

Dudley is obviously pleased to have Robert Mann's interest and affection. "Knowing him is a great thing for me," comments Dudley. "He's given me enormous support and encouragement. He's the one person who has encouraged me over and over again to play in public with him, and I'm very, very grateful. The main problem is practice. That's all you have to do—apply yourself. Bobby's support and encouragement has been total, and now I fear the classical community a lot less than I did. At first, I had real inhibitions about technique and the whole classical music world, not realizing that if you work at it, technique can be acquired. Bobby made me realize I *can* play and enjoy that sense of fulfillment like anybody else."

Robert Mann himself is happy to talk about Dudley's classical playing. "He's a very good musician," Mann affirms. "He can sight-read anything, and he's very sensitive. In my view, Dudley could easily be a third-stream composer, using jazz as well as classical elements. He's also an excellent chamber music player. When I first brought him the Beethoven, he sight-read it, and he had the technique to play it as well! So I kept after him, and he finally agreed to do it at Carnegie Hall. But if he had to choose between classical music and jazz, he'd choose jazz, I have no doubt. And you know, he actually got me to like Erroll Garner!"

Dudley gets a faraway look in his eyes when he talks about some of his ambitious projects for the future. "I want to do the Haydn violin and piano duets," he declares. "It would be nice if I could acquire a small repertoire. I just bought myself some Rachmaninoff preludes, and I'm going to have fun getting into those. And then I want to do some more Bach and Scarlatti, and to play some Mozart, too. It's a real challenge to get that evenness that is so essential in Mozart."

As Dudley's public image continues to grow and flourish, he has the power to turn his film-going public on to his music. Perhaps his dedication and total sincerity will lead some movie fans to take a new interest in the musical Moore. If so, it would make him very happy. Watching Dudley as he played, I got the feeling that he would enjoy working more as a jazz musician. He talks animatedly about opening a restaurant with some friends in which he would play solo piano, and I have no doubt that he *will* do that! It seems that he can do anything he wants. Right now he is having great success with *all* his projects, and, best yet, he seems happy with his life and with himself.

Our afternoon of taping went very smoothly. Dudley is a wonderful guest—easy-going, charming, great fun as a two-piano partner, and, of course, never at a loss for a word or a sly musical interpolation. I wish we could have included his special arrangements of "Colonel Bogey" and "Die Flabbergast"—maybe next time.

1983

POSTSCRIPT

At the time that I wrote this article about Dudley, he was tremendously active in many fields. He was making new films, one after another, and had given several classical concerts, which were highly successful. However, at that point he decided to take a two-year hiatus, although his earlier movies were still seen often enough on cable TV to keep him in the public eye.

For a while he was back in the swing of things, looking over film scripts, trying out his new Boesendorfer piano, and experimenting with various computers designed to instantly reproduce his improvisations in manuscript form. When he tired of these activities he enjoyed sitting in on piano at some of his favorite hangouts. When the pressure was on again, Dudley claimed that he yearned for more free time, but the demands of his profession held him in thrall, and it was obvious he was loving every minute of it.

Unfortunately, all the activities that Dudley was getting into seemed to fail, including a television comedy series that was not successful. He played piano concertos with some symphony orchestras, yet somehow one was aware that all was not well with Dudley. He had remarried and had a child, but shortly thereafter he and his wife were divorced, and rumors were rampant about his drinking. Once in a while, however, one of Dudley's great films such as *Arthur* or *10* would be shown again on TV, reminding people of his comic genius. It is sad that someone who was so hilariously funny and at the same time a really fine musician could in reality be an unhappy person, leading a tragic life.

People began to wonder what was really going on with Dudley Moore. Then the news broke that he was suffering from progressive supranuclear palsy, an incurable brain disorder that affected his speech and motion. Many who had thought that Dudley was an alcoholic finally became aware that it was actually the degenerative disease that was causing him to slur his speech and lose his balance. It is a great tragedy that such a thing could happen to this wonderfully gifted and sensitive individual.

For a while he was receiving treatment at a rehabilitation center and was being cared for by loving friends, but on March 27, 2002, he succumbed to this insidious disease. One can only wish that the medical profession had discovered a cure in time for Dudley to regain his marvelous skill and be once again the jovial and endearing guy that I knew for so many years. We all miss him terribly.

12

The Untold Story
of the International
Sweethearts of Rhythm

The theater was ablaze with lights that proclaimed THE INTERNATIONAL SWEETHEARTS OF RHYTHM. The Sweethearts, an all-woman sixteen-piece band, were familiar to the tough, show-wise audience, and a long line of eagerly expectant people stretched down the street and around the comer, waiting for the doors to open. Known to the audience as the finest all-girl jazz band in the country, the Sweethearts had in seven years attained a reputation equal to that of the great male bands of the period, those led by Jimmie Lunceford, Count Basie, and Fletcher Henderson. The year was 1945; the place, the Apollo Theatre in Harlem.

A hot attraction, the Sweethearts were then at the height of their fame, although to some they were merely a novelty—sixteen pretty girl musicians led by an extravagantly beautiful young woman, Anna Mae Winburn. They played with assurance, discipline, and excitement, reflecting the expert teaching of their director, Maurice King. There were some fine

The International Sweethearts of Rhythm, 1942.

soloists, including Violet (Vi) Burnside, a driving, gutty tenor sax player with more than a suggestion of Coleman Hawkins in her style. The star soloist of the trumpet section was Ray Carter, whose muted sound was colorful and technically brilliant. The hard-swinging drummer, Pauline Braddy, inspired by her idol and mentor Big Sid Catlett, whipped the band along with a strong rhythm. Her foot beating on the bass drum pedal matched exactly the time-keeping of the bassist, Margaret (Trump) Gibson, and together they gave solid, dependable backing to the soloists.

The main attraction was roly-poly Ernestine (Tiny) Davis, billed as "245 Lbs. of Solid Jive and Rhythm." A compelling personality, she had a distinct flair for comedy and a humorous way with a song. Her comic dancing, rolling eyes, and hilarious rendition of "Stompin' the Blues" broke up the audience, and she played a strong, forceful trumpet on "I Can't Get Started," another crowd-pleaser.

The band played at the beginning of each show (four a day), and again later in the show. There were other name acts on the bill, but the Sweethearts opened and closed the program.

This band was truly unique in that it was a racially mixed group, a phenomenon unheard of even in blasé New York City. They were known to have traveled widely in the South and Midwest, many miles from their starting point, the Piney Woods Country Life School near Jackson, Mississippi, where the original band was formed in 1938. The members of that first band were all approximately fourteen or fifteen years old, high-spirited, naive youngsters who enjoyed playing for dances in small towns within driving distance of the school.

Between 1938 and the present date at the Apollo, the band's personnel had changed many times. Ione and Irene Gresham, who both played sax with the original band, had decided to stay at Piney Woods when the band turned professional; this was a decision reached by several of the girls. Others had concluded that life on the road was not for them; still others had left the band to get married. However, some of the members of the original group remained—Helen Jones and Ina Belle Byrd, trombone; Willie Mae Lee Wong, baritone sax; Edna Williams, trumpet and vocals; Johnnie Mae Rice, piano; and Pauline Braddy, drums. Inside the theater the girls were dressing and warming up on their instruments. Tiny Davis practiced high notes on the trumpet, getting ready for her feature numbers. Anna Mae Winburn gave final touches to her sleek, upswept hairdo. She wore an exquisite, tightly fitted sequin gown, while the band members were dressed in decorous black skirts and jackets, with white blouses. Each girl wore a flower in her hair, which added a feminine touch to her rather severe attire. Mrs. Rae Lee Jones was the manager of the band, a tall, imposing woman and a disciplinarian reminiscent of a boarding school matron. She walked among the girls, adjusting a neckline here, tucking in a stray hair there, checking the girls' lipstick and eye make-up. "That'll do; off you go," she ordered. With a last-minute flurry of practice notes, the girls filed out of the dressing room to take their places on stage.

The huge curtain parted as strains of the Sweethearts' theme song, featuring Rosalind (Roz) Cron on alto sax, filled the theater. Next, a solid, swinging arrangement of "Tuxedo Junction" kept the audience snapping their fingers. Among the several outstanding soloists featured on the program was diminutive Evelyn McGee, who drew whistles of appreciation for her singing of "Candy" and "Rum and Coca Cola." Anna Mae Winburn put aside her baton to sing "Do You Want to Jump, Children?" "Yeah, yeah," shrilled the band, answering her musical question in childlike voices. Following this was a wild, frantic version of "Sweet Georgia Brown" taken at an impossible tempo, with Vi Burnside freewheeling in and around the melody, playing a shower of notes on her tenor sax that took one's breath away. When the show was over, and with the echoes of the cheers and applause still ringing in their ears, the girls could now look forward to a quick snack between shows, visits from friends, and the heady excitement of being back in New York City.

Few white people ever saw the Sweethearts. At that time the Apollo and other theaters like it—the Howard in Washington, the Regal in Chicago, the Paradise in Detroit—catered to black audiences, and the small number of whites who ventured there were the real jazz aficionados. Among them was record producer John Hammond, who thought the band was "just marvelous; a great band." It might even have been, as one of the fans remarked, "the world's greatest girl dance band." Pianist Earl "Fatha" Hines had high praise for the group—"a wonderful swinging bunch of gals"—but there were negative comments, too. Huffed one well-known woman player when asked if she had ever worked with the Sweethearts, "You wouldn't catch me anywhere near *that* band." And the typical remark from male musicians was, "You certainly couldn't consider them in the same league as any good *male* band." Yet musical director Maurice King was enthusiastic. "You could put those girls behind a curtain and people would be convinced it was men playing." The group was often likened to the Lunceford band, and Jimmie Lunceford himself had high praise for the girls.

It had taken stamina, long hours of practice, dedication, and experiences both rewarding and frustrating to bring the International Sweethearts of Rhythm all the way from Piney Woods, Mississippi, to the Apollo Theatre in New York. The newer band members were all aware of the pioneering spirit that had helped the first schoolgirl band to pave the way for the present group's highly acclaimed reputation.

Research indicates that the principal of Piney Woods Country Life School, Laurence C. Jones, was a most unusual man—well educated (University of Iowa), charming, knowledgeable in the ways of the world, and totally committed to raising money for the betterment of his school. Money was constantly needed to take care of the thousand boys and girls, many of them orphans, who lived at the school.

Mr. Jones believed in keeping everybody working. The bell rang at 5:00 A.M.; at six the children had breakfast; and by seven they were all busy with school work or some other activity. There was a farm—boys were taught farming and furniture-making among other things—and the girls learned domestic skills such as cooking and dressmaking. The football team bested everyone in the area, and there were two marching bands, one of boys, one of girls. The school had everything—there never had been a place like it for blacks in the South. At that time they were held back, yet Mr. Jones's powers of persuasion were so strong that he was able to convince the white businessmen whom he met that his idea of teaching every child a trade was of prime importance. He knew the right people to approach, and money flowed into the school from many sources.

There was a great deal of musical activity before the formation of the Sweethearts. In addition to the forty-five-piece marching bands, there was a group called the "Cotton Blossom Singers," who were at that time the main fund-raisers for the school. Mr. Jones personally supervised all these activities.

This was the burgeoning swing era—the great bands of Ellington, Hines, Basie, and Lunceford were developing unique stylings from their jazz heritage. A new kind of jazz, jazz people could dance to, began to flourish, and it burst forth all over the country, inspiring white musicians—the Dorsey Brothers, Benny Goodman, Artie Shaw, Glenn Miller—

to form their own bands. It was inevitable that someone would think of putting together a different type of show business package, one that was bound to succeed—an all-girl (white) swing band, Ina Ray Hutton and Her Melodears. Irving Mills, mentor of the Ellington band, did just that.

According to Helen Jones, who had been adopted at the age of three months by Laurence Jones and his wife and brought up at Piney Woods, Mr. Jones heard Ina Ray and her band in Chicago, and his fertile mind instantly grasped the possibilities and advantages of establishing such a group to raise funds for Piney Woods. As soon as he returned, he set about selecting girls for the band. There were many who had musical talent and who, with training, would develop into competent musicians. Helen Jones recalls that Mr. Jones wanted her to play the violin, but she begged for a chance to learn the trombone, because she "loved to watch that slide going in and out." This was a fortunate decision, because Helen's strong, full tone enhanced the Sweethearts' trombone section from the formation of the group until they disbanded.

No one remembers who was the first director of the band. After Laurence Jones had assembled the group, they were rehearsed for a short time by a teacher named Lawrence Jefferson. Then Edna Williams, a talented young pianist and trumpet player not much older than the band members themselves, took over. It seems that Edna Williams, or someone like her, taught the girls their first tunes, which were, according to drummer Pauline Braddy, "Baby, Don't Tell on Me," "How Long, Baby," "720 in the Books," and "Star Dust." Some of the girls were given half notes or whole notes to play, while others played the melody. A few learned the tunes by reading the music, while the others would imitate notes and phrases sung or played by the teacher. She also taught them breath control and how to produce a tone. Gradually they became proficient enough to move on to "stocks"—published orchestrations of popular tunes of the day. Finally, they were ready to set forth on a fund-raising trip in the area as Mr. Jones had envisioned. Sixteen in all, the girls rode in a special bus to play dates in armories, halls, and high school gymnasiums. Mr. Jones thought of everything. He even hired a chaperone, Mrs. Ella P. Gant, who traveled along with the girls.

As the girls gained in experience and proficiency, the band blossomed. The plain blouses and dark skirts the girls wore gave them a fresh appearance. Their neatly combed hair and well-scrubbed faces emphasized how young they were to be on the road. Soon the trips became longer, and Mr. Jones hired Vivian Crawford as tutor for the girls and Mrs. Rae Lee Jones (no relation) to replace Mrs. Gant. Mrs. Jones was a social worker from Omaha, whom Laurence Jones had met on one of his fund-raising trips. She kept order among the girls and brooked no disobedience but was concerned enough about their health to see that they all ate well and drank plenty of milk.

By now the band was beginning to sound more professional. Some of the original group had dropped out, and others took their places. Evelyn McGee, a talented youngster from Anderson, South Carolina, joined the band as vocalist. Mr. Jones had an uncanny way of spotting talent. On a trip with the band to Bolivar, Mississippi, he espied a very beautiful girl, Helen Saine, playing basketball and invited her to come to Piney Woods and join the band. "But I can't play an instrument," said Helen. "We'll teach you," Mr. Jones replied. Something in his approach must have made the invitation seem worthwhile to her parents, because Helen Saine was allowed to leave immediately for Piney Woods and was soon learning to play tenor and alto sax.

Then came Grace Bayron and her sister, Judy. While on a trip to New York the year before, Laurence Jones had noticed Gracie carrying her saxophone case on an East Harlem street. He followed her home and asked her parents if they would relocate their family to Piney Woods—Mr. Bayron to teach Spanish, Gracie and Judy to play in the band. The parents declined the offer, but by some strange quirk of fate both died within the same year. Remembering Laurence Jones's invitation, Gracie Bayron telephoned him soon after her parents' death. Arrangements were made, and a few days later a chaperone arrived to escort the girls to

Piney Woods. "Gracie started playing in the band right away," Judy Bayron recalls. "I was just given a guitar to hold so I could sit in the rhythm section. But eventually I learned to play trombone."

The band began to take on an air of professionalism that Rae Lee Jones helped to bring about with her constant supervision and strict rules. She had insisted that each girl wear a flower in her hair onstage. Now she started buying costumes for them that gave them a more sophisticated appearance.

Hotel accommodations for a racially mixed group were impossible to find, so trips were made in a bus fitted with bunk beds so that the group could travel all night and wake up refreshed. They ate on the bus, practiced, prepared their lessons, got dressed, and, as the bus pulled into town, were ready in their costumes for their performance. It would seem as if the Sweethearts led an exciting life, traveling from town to town, playing to packed houses and appreciative audiences, but in fact it was a hard, rugged existence, with no chance for social life. The girls looked glamorous onstage, but, says Helen Jones, "We were the biggest bunch of virgins in America."

The band's fund-raising endeavors took them farther and farther afield, and in October 1939 they played Chicago, Des Moines, Omaha, and Kansas City in the space of a week. Their Chicago appearance was sponsored by the Chicago Piney Woods Club, and a review of their performance at the Romping Earl's Club House read in part:

"Sixteen girls, best known in music circles as the 'International Sweethearts of Rhythm' who hail from Piney Woods, Mississippi, right in the heart of the Delta, invaded Chicago Saturday night and gave jitterbugs, swing fans and hep cats something to talk about.

"They beat out a bit of mellow jive, sang the latest song hits, then started a swing session that caused the dance lovers to stop in their tracks and listen to the hot sounds that blared out from the instruments played by these Mississippi girls.

"Together for two years, these girls handle their instruments like veterans and can rightfully take a place among the leading male aggregations."

Perhaps reviews such as this helped to pique the interest of a talent promoter from Washington, D.C., for Daniel M. Gary suddenly appeared on the scene, approaching Mrs. Jones with the suggestion that he take over the bookings for the band. It seems that after consulting with Laurence Jones, Mr. Gary did indeed start booking the band, and they embarked on their most successful tour thus far, playing major cities in the South and Midwest.

However, as their musicianship improved and their successes increased, so in direct proportion did their problems—problems that would soon lead to a decision that would drastically affect the future of the band and its members.

It appears that Laurence Jones thought he was losing control of the band, primarily because Rae Lee Jones was encouraging the girls to question his judgment in financial and other matters. He therefore confronted her with the threat of dismissal. When the girls decided to stand by her, he informed them that they would not receive their high school diplomas unless they returned to Piney Woods immediately. To his dismay, the girls refused to change their minds; even his adopted daughter, Helen, defied him. Perhaps they had already been influenced in their decision by thoughts of the bright future Dan Gary had promised them.

It was a momentous decision, especially since everyone knew they were virtually running away from Piney Woods, taking with them the uniforms and instruments belonging to the school as well as the bus. Perhaps the consequences of such a decision had not yet dawned on them—that Mr. Jones, hurt and furious at what he thought was a betrayal, would later have Rae Lee Jones arrested for theft. Even this did not stop the forward movement of the band, because Dan Gary, through his various political connections, managed to secure her release on the condition that the bus, uniforms, and instruments be returned to Piney Woods.

At this point, having lost Piney Woods as home base, the band needed a new headquarters. Property records show that Rae Lee Jones, as trustee of the International Sweethearts of Rhythm, Inc., purchased a ten-room house at 908 South Quinn Street, Arlington, Virginia. The girls believed they were members of the corporation and that they owned shares in the house, as they had been told that a portion of their salaries would be used to help pay the mortgage. It was a beautiful idea—their very own house where they could rest and relax. To girls who had started in the band with nothing, the prospect of having their own house was thrilling indeed.

Once settled in Arlington, the girls rehearsed every day, sometimes for as long as six hours at a stretch, and consequently their playing became more polished. They began to believe that their dreams of hitting the big time would come true when they were plunged into the exciting, fast-moving, sometimes sinister web of black nightclubs while continuing to play at well-known ballrooms and theaters. There were more changes in the band personnel—stronger, more experienced musicians were brought in. Anna Mae Winburn, who had once led a group of her own, was hired to front the band; her beauty and stage presence were a definite asset. She brought down the house with her rendition of "Blow-top Blues," a song written for her by jazz critic Leonard Feather.

It was becoming quite evident that despite the many changes and improvements in the band, their repertoire was too limited for the bookings Dan Gary had scheduled for them at theaters such as the Apollo, the Howard Theater in Washington, D.C., the Regal in Chicago, and other top-rated theaters across the country. It was time to bring in an arranger, and Mrs. Jones was advised to hire Eddie Durham, who had been prominent in the Count Basie Band and who was also well known as a songwriter, guitarist, and trombone player. He had to his credit a hit song, "I Don't Want to Set the World on Fire," and other original tunes. His arrangements of "St. Louis Blues" and "At Sundown" were simple but effective. He also arranged a beautiful Harold Arlen song, "When the Sun Comes Out," as well as some of his own compositions, "Moten Swing" and "Topsy," for the Sweethearts. Durham had had his own all-woman band, so he knew the best approach to take in teaching the Sweethearts. Knowing that there were few improvisors in the band, he wrote out solos for them that sounded as if they were improvised on the spot when played.

Durham had high regard for the Sweethearts, and he enjoyed working with them. "People couldn't believe it was women playing," he commented, "so sometimes when the curtain opened I'd make off that I was playing and the girls were just pantomiming. Then I'd stop, and people could see they really were playing. I simplified things for them as much as possible. You structure arrangements for people . . . you write for what you've got. I had to train the Sweethearts, but at the Apollo nobody believed girls could play that way."

Durham showed considerable sensitivity in allowing for the girls' technical limitations while stressing their strong points. He played an important role, as a teacher as well as an arranger, in the development of the band. Through his efforts they were beginning to know where they were going musically.

None of the surviving members of the band's early day recalls exactly when their romantic fantasies of success ran head-long into reality. They were becoming aware that real life was turning out to be not only places like the Apollo but also endless and grueling one-nighters, tedious rehearsals, and long nights on the bus. They sometimes had to eat in dirty restaurants where often they were handed their food through a back window, typical treatment for blacks in the South at that time. (Anna Mae Winburn recalls screaming angrily at one restaurant owner, "My brother is overseas fighting for people like you, and you're treating me this way?")

Most of the time the girls slept on the bus because it was too risky for mixed groups to stay in black hotels. On the rare occasion that they did, there was always the danger that the police would question the hotel owner, trying to find out if some of the girls were white. Ironically, the white girls, and those who looked white, suffered as much from southern racism as the black band members.

The girls were harassed in hotels and restaurants and even while on stage. Policemen would roam the clubs, trying to spot the white band members. Often they succeeded despite the heavy, dark make-up the lighter-skinned girls used in an attempt to disguise their pale complexions and the wigs they wore to hide their light hair. When this happened, Mrs. Jones was ready with false credentials to prove the girls were Negro. It was a constant worry in the minds of the girls that, despite all their precautions, one of their number might be taken away at any time, not for any wrongdoing but simply because of her color.

Harassment of another sort was experienced by some of the black band members. During a performance in a nightclub, Anna Mae Winburn tripped while stepping onto the stage. When a white man rose to help her, he was immediately forced back into his seat by a nearby policeman who ordered, "You sit down and let that nigger woman help herself."

(A few years later Anna Mae and her husband, Duke Pilgrim, fared better in a confrontation with southern police. While driving through town with two white members of the band they had formed, their car was stopped by a policeman. "You know you're not supposed to have them white women in the car," rasped the officer. Pilgrim, with a look of innocence, replied, "I know that, officer, that's why I've got them sitting in the *back* seat." He drove away, leaving the befuddled policeman standing there.)

The band kept improving, kept moving ahead. They had seen their names on theater marquees and billboards, and they had heard the warm applause of audiences all over the country.

Their next big milestone musically was the hiring of Jesse Stone as the band's coach-arranger. Like Eddie Durham, Stone was a highly respected and successful figure in the world of topflight Negro swing bands. He had written several well-known songs, "Idaho" and "Smack Dab in the Middle" being the most familiar.

Jesse Stone made many changes and improvements in the band. He brought in several new musicians, among them Lucille Dixon, bass; Marjorie Pettiford (Oscar's sister), alto sax; Johnnie Mae (Tex) Stansbury, trumpet; Amy Garrison, sax; and Roxanna Lucas, guitar. The addition of these talented women, whose reading and playing skill was at an advanced level, raised the caliber of the entire group. He made a special point of teaching the girls how to improve their intonation, how to listen to each other in order to achieve a smooth blend and a sharp attack. Some of his new arrangements were more challenging than anything the girls had attempted thus far, and therefore special coaching was necessary.

The major innovation that Stone made was the formation of a singing group drawn from the band. Helen Jones recalls, "We had some numbers where a group of us went down front and sang. Evelyn, Ella Ritz Lucas, somebody else and myself had a quartet. We went down front after we played part of the show, and we sang and everybody liked it. Jesse is really the one who did that. In fact, we sang some of his numbers."

During Jesse Stone's first year with the band the Sweethearts made considerable musical progress. The overall sound was smoother, the musicianship improving. It was a rough life but a free one to the extent that the girls had broken loose from familial ties, from school and similar restraints. Also, the earlier camaraderie had grown into a bond of friendship that had been strengthened by the many experiences, good and bad, that the girls had shared.

But not only did the band members learn more about music from Jesse Stone, they also became fully aware through him that they were performing for less than adequate wages.

Evelyn McGee recalls, "Jesse would fight with Mrs. Jones about how she was taking advantage of the girls. For example, we played five shows a day in Baltimore during Christmas week. The lines were unbelievable, the audiences fantastic—but at the end of the week Mrs. Jones gave each girl less than $100.

"Jesse hit the ceiling and gave his notice. But Mrs. Jones held him to his two-year contract, so he stayed on another year. When he finally left, it wasn't because he was dissatisfied with the band. It was because of the treatment we were getting from Rae Lee Jones."

The girls were becoming disenchanted, and some of them left. Those who stayed on seemed to have a more philosophical attitude about things. "It's funny, when you're young and don't know anything, you do a lot of things without thinking," Helen Jones reflected recently. "You believe a lot of things people tell you when you're 'country' and don't know much about the world. I can see how certain people kept control of our destiny then. Deep down, we knew we weren't making much money, and we knew the hotels were dirty and the food was bad. But we didn't think about that so much—we were enjoying ourselves."

The year was 1944; the Americans had been involved in the Second World War for three years. Perhaps because many male musicians had been drafted, all-girl orchestras proliferated and flourished. Among them the groups directed by Phil Spitalny, Ina Ray Hutton, and Ada Leonard were best known, but all the girl bands were more in demand than they had ever been before.

Not only were the Sweethearts busy, they were perhaps more stable, since there were fewer changes of personnel that year. One notable change was the replacement of Marge Pettiford as lead alto by Rosalind (Roz) Cron, a Jewish girl from Boston, Massachusetts. Roz had been with Ada Leonard's band for some time. There were violins in that band, and the music was more sedate. Consequently Roz, a high-spirited girl who was an extremely good player, relished the freer, more swinging style of the Sweethearts.

"I remember something about the difference between working for Ada Leonard and being with the Sweethearts," Roz says. "In all the theaters, when the Sweethearts started playing the audience would come in, dancing down the aisles to their seats. Black audiences were always like that. But if you'd go to hear Tommy or Jimmy Dorsey, or Ada Leonard, people just *walked* to their seats and sat down."

Shortly after Roz Cron joined the band, Maurice King arrived from

Detroit to replace Jesse Stone as musical director. He had a cataclysmic effect on the band. Roz Cron in particular was impressed. "Maurice immediately put us through the most grueling rehearsals. It was a tough struggle, but we made it. 'Tuxedo Junction' turned into a really polished thing."

Maurice King recalls, "When I worked with the girls I would show them a passage in an arrangement and how to phrase it, four bars at a time. We'd keep on going over it, and finally, when it jelled, you could see their little eyes beam. It was like putting an erector set together."

King obviously enjoyed teaching and working with the girls. He began writing specialty numbers for the band, and his "Vi Vigor," "Slightly Frantic," "Don't Get It Twisted," and "Diggin' Dirt" became part of the Sweethearts' book. "'Diggin' Dirt' was what we called a dance-stopper," said King. "We'd end the tune, pause, and then start it all over again. We'd do this several times. It was a big number."

En route to California, where they were scheduled to record for the Armed Forces Radio Network, the girls spent their days playing, rehearsing, and sleeping on the bus. Finally, they reached Texas, where they were booked on a series of nightclub dates. One afternoon in Austin a policeman who was watching them rehearse asked King, "Isn't that a white girl over there?" "What makes you think she's white?" King replied. Looking right at Roz Cron, the policeman said, "Well, she looks white to me." At this point King answered piously, rolling his eyes heavenward, "Well, our girls are not responsible for what one of their parents may have been forced to do." He then turned back to the band and continued the rehearsal, while Roz, red as a beet, had a difficult time keeping quiet.

Once in California the girls were plunged into a round of new activities. They were taken to various Hollywood studios to make short films which would later be used as "fillers" in movie theaters. Most of these are now in the collections of jazz buffs.

At this time the Sweethearts also recorded several shows live at the Club Alabam for the GIs in Europe and the Pacific, each show featuring a big star. It was thrilling for the Sweethearts to work with such people as Ethel Waters, Lena Horne, Jerry Colonna, Phil Harris, and Jimmy Durante. Recently, portions of these programs have surfaced in a collection of women's jazz performances on a small, independent label. Many of these "air checks" are also being sold on the open market, so there is no telling where the music of the Sweethearts may be heard next.

After playing the Club Plantation in Los Angeles, one of the best West Coast jazz clubs, the group set forth once again for Arlington, Virginia. A whole new chain of events was beginning. The State Department had become interested in the band because there had been a demand for it from the GIs in Europe, who had heard the broadcasts over the Armed Forces Radio Network. This resulted in a tour of Europe with USO Camp Shows for the Sweethearts.

Attired in their brand new USO uniforms, the Sweethearts sailed for Europe on July 15, 1945, reaching Le Havre on July 22. They were chaperoned by Maurice King, as Rae Lee Jones had become ill and couldn't make the trip. In the European Theatre the war was already over, but there were still thousands of GIs in the Occupational Forces to be entertained. When the girls arrived, they were ecstatically received, and every time the band performed the audiences went wild. The program varied somewhat from the routine they used in nightclubs. Tunes were added that the GIs knew and liked, but basically it was the same show that had excited the Apollo audience earlier that year.

They were all living together in a hotel, and Maurice King was required to conduct a room check at 10:30 P.M. every night because of the curfew. He would make the room check and leave, knowing full well that some of the girls would sneak out afterwards. "I should have received a medal for bringing back that band intact," King has said with a mysterious smile. Piney Woods seemed a million light years away.

When the band returned to the States after Christmas 1945, the girls had money in the bank for the first time in their lives. As financial guardian of the band, Maurice King had seen to it that most of the money the girls earned was deposited in U.S. banks to await their return from Europe. Only Helen Jones had elected to have Rae Lee Jones hold her money for safekeeping instead of depositing it in a bank.

The controlling factors of the band were still the Washingtonians, Dan Gary and his partner, Al Dade. Gary was still the president of the corporation, and Rae Lee Jones was still the trustee, although she had left Arlington to return to her hometown of Omaha, seriously ill.

The band went on. More and different projects were being undertaken. Leonard Feather, who has always admired women musicians and done his best to further their careers, now prepared to record for RCA Victor, using different women's groups. The Sweethearts recorded two numbers for Leonard Feather—"Don't Get It Twisted" and "Vi Vigor," both written by Maurice King. They also made two sides for Guild Records, with one side featuring Tiny Davis singing and playing "Stompin' the Blues." The reverse side spotlighted Anna Mae Winburn singing "Do You Want to Jump, Children?" The culmination of all this activity was a short film, *That Man of Mine*, which starred Ruby Dee and featured the Sweethearts. Maurice King wrote the theme song, and the Sweethearts played it.

At last the Sweethearts had realized some of their earlier dreams. They had played to audiences of thousands in the United States and abroad, recorded overseas broadcasts with big-name Hollywood stars, had made records and films. What was left for them?

For some it seemed a good time to leave the band and go back to school. Others had already met their future husbands, and they left to get married. A few stayed on, but there were many new girls coming in. Some remained for a while, but others left after only a week or two, so it is impossible to document all the band members during the last years the group was together. Nevertheless, the band continued to grow in stature. Some of the musicians were the best the band had ever had, and this is confirmed by the following enthusiastic review carried in the July

27, 1946, issue of *Billboard*. Noting the band's appearance at the Million Dollar in Los Angeles, the review read in part:

"The joint is jumpin' again this week with a solid bill headlined by the International Sweethearts of Rhythm . . . Anna Mae Winburn fronts the Sweethearts (all-gal ork) in smooth and easy style. Fem musikers are top instrumentalists and dish out a polished brand of music, offering such widely titled concoctions as 'Don't Get It Twisted' and 'Just the Thing.' Instrumental breaks fall to Pauline Braddy on the skins and a sensational sax tooter, Vi Burnside. Latter socked 'em between the eyes with 'After You've Gone' and 'I Cover the Waterfront.'

"In the vocal bracket, featured thrush Mildred McIver does 'Day by Day' and 'Mr. Postman Blues' well. . . . Surprise vocal shot was guitarist Carline Ray doing 'Temptation.' Gal has a deep voice and knows how to peddle a tune."

The band was to continue until the end of 1948, playing brilliantly and getting excellent reviews. And yet, something was missing now that virtually all the original Sweethearts had left.

Helen Jones was on her way back to Omaha to visit Rae Lee Jones, now desperately ill. It was a shock to Helen to see her so obviously near death, but just as shocking was the admission Mrs. Jones made—that she had spent all the money Helen had entrusted to her. She begged Helen's forgiveness. "I didn't realize the magnitude of it until years later," Helen reflected recently. "I felt so sorry for her. There she was, down and out, in this little old house that she had bought for her parents. And when she died she left it to me, but I didn't take it. Her parents were still there, and I didn't want to put them out. So there was nothing I could do. At that time I was young, and I didn't know anything, so whatever came up, I just accepted it. That's life—everyone learns one way or another."

Somehow, in spite of the mystery surrounding the management of the band, Rae Lee Jones had been the life force that held it together. When she died, the band also died.

But memories and dreams do not die easily. They still flourish in the hearts and minds of these women, who open their scrapbooks and point with pride to the fresh-faced group of girls with whom they once had shared so much. No matter that their moment in the spotlight was brief. Their spirit and courage has been passed on to a new generation of talented young women who are seeking their own dreams.

1980

POSTSCRIPT

Talking as I often do with different members of the Sweethearts, I realize how well they have managed their lives since the breakup of the band. Many of them went to college and embarked on new careers; some got married and raised families, emerging from their show business lives to become conservative, responsible, caring citizens.

In 1980 the members of the Sweethearts were specially flown from their homes in various parts of the country to appear at the Kansas City Women's Jazz Festival. It was the first time they had seen one another since the band broke up years before, and it was heartwarming to see the affection these women have for each other and their excitement at getting together to be honored by the Festival Committee.

Since that time, there have been many changes. Sadly, some of the members of the band have passed away—the beautiful and glamorous Anna Mae Winburn, who thrilled listeners with her singing, is one of them. A few years ago I was playing a date in Lexington, Kentucky, and Anna Mae and her daughter came to the concert. It was wonderful to see them, and we talked for hours, catching up on her life and family. That was the last time I saw her. Tiny Davis was still entertaining with her trumpet and songs in clubs around Chicago until a few years ago, when she had a fatal heart attack. Pauline Braddy, the energetic and hard-swinging drummer, is also gone.

Evelyn McGee, the effervescent singer, was with the band from the beginning. She was married to songwriter Jesse Stone for many years, and after the breakup of the band they performed in clubs until 1998, when Jesse passed away after a short illness. Now in her eighties, Evelyn is still recording and singing up a storm! Helen Saine, the beautiful and talented alto saxophone player, is unfortunately confined to a nursing home. Roz Cron, who for many years worked in an office, has retired and taken up the clarinet again with renewed vigor. She is still a member of the Musicians' Union in Los Angeles and is keeping up with the musical scene there. Trombonist Helen Jones Woods still lives comfortably in Omaha;

her daughter, Kathy, is a well-known television producer in Washington, D.C.; her son, Michael, is a doctor in Los Angeles.

Roz and I talk on the phone quite often, and I also speak to Helen Woods occasionally. It means a great deal to me to keep in touch with the band members, most of whom I came to know very well when I was interviewing them for this article. Unfortunately, we haven't seen each other face to face since the festival in Kansas City. For a while after that there was some interest in doing a documentary on the band, but somehow that has never come to fruition, and now, with their members somewhat depleted, there is less likelihood of putting a film together. However, much has been written about the band by various writers, and young women musicians have become interested in their story. The Sweethearts blazed a trail, taking hardship and prejudice in their stride, and their story should be an inspiration to the jazzwomen of today.

13 Alec Wilder: The Compleat Composer

Alec Wilder's music has been a part of my life for many years. As a teenager, long before I left England for the United States, I listened to his now legendary Octets—comprising harpsichord, clarinet, bass clarinet, bassoon, oboe, bass, drums, and flute—and was intrigued by the fascinating combination of classical melodies, graceful and light, that were played with a jazz beat. The pieces had style, elegance, and wit. Some of them were tender, some humorous; all had imaginative, sometimes puzzling titles—"Jack, This Is My Husband," "The House Detective Registers," "The Children Met the Train," "It's Silk, Feel It," and so on. All were short and perfectly put together. The melodies were so intricately woven between the various instruments that it was hard for me to pick out the main themes on the piano; I would just listen to the records and let my imagination run riot.

Gradually I absorbed more Wilder music from the BBC. "I'll Be Around" was a song that became popular in England, and "While We're

Alec Wilder and Marian McPartland, 1976. (Photo by Louis Ouzer)

Young" was another. I never saw the sheet music. I just soaked up the melodies from hearing them. I've always gravitated toward harmonically intricate tunes with tender, romantic lyrics. Later, after I came to the United States, I learned more Wilder compositions. Then, when we were at the Hickory House in 1953, I recorded "I'll Be Around" in a baroque style, with harp and cello, for Capitol. I never knew Alec had heard it and liked it until years later.

We first met at the Hickory House in the 1950s, but it was just a brief meeting, and years later, when I was playing at The Apartment, I saw Alec sitting at the bar, quietly listening. After the set I slipped onto a stool beside him, and we chatted. He had a record of the Swingle Singers under his arm, and several books, which I later came to know were standard equipment with him. "Gosh, I'm dying to hear that record," I said enviously. "Take it, dear," he said. He pulled out a fountain pen (a *real* pen with a nib!) and autographed it. I went home thinking how generous and pleasant he had been. I've since found out he likes to share things—books, ideas, stories, and even his friends!

A year or so later I saw him again. I was in the airport in Rochester, New York. Alec was there at the bar, deep in a book. I wanted to say hello but didn't dare. He looked forbidding and austere, and he had no idea I was watching him. As I boarded the plane, he was already seated (in first class), still reading, still, to me, quite unapproachable. I went on back into the coach section.

I didn't see him again for several years, until I was playing at the Rountowner Motel in Rochester—Alec's birthplace. Someone mentioned Alec was in town. I impulsively called his hotel and left a message—"Please ring me, and let's get together." The next day I heard from him, and we arranged to meet that night for dinner. Alec is a great conversationalist and very humorous. He laughs a lot, and he made me laugh as we discussed music and musicians, songs we like, gossip, our mutual friends. It was delightful.

Then the band got ready to play. It was a Hawaiian group. Alec's face took on a pained expression as the musicians tuned up. I started to giggle. "Let's get out of here," we both said at once. He signaled wildly for the check. I never thought two people could gobble down dessert, gulp coffee, and tear out of a restaurant so fast. "I *hate* that damned Hawaiian music," he said.

He came to hear my trio at The Rountowner. He evidently liked what he heard, for he kept coming back night after night. Sometimes he brought faculty members from the Eastman School or his close friend, photographer Louis Ouzer. One night as he was leaving he said, "I'm going to write a piece for you—I'll bring it in this week." I was pleased, but didn't really believe him. I forgot all about it until the next time he showed up at The Rountowner. He airily tossed me a sheet of music, on which was written, "Jazz Waltz for a Friend—a small present from Alec Wilder."

I was delighted, and I couldn't wait to play the piece. It had a haunting melody which had a way of turning back on itself that I found fascinating. It was deceptively simple to play yet hard to memorize and to improvise on. Many of Alec's pieces are that way, but they are rewarding, for as you delve into them and explore their intricacies, you find fresh ways to go. "Jazz Waltz for a Friend" became a part of our trio repertoire, just as Alec became part of my audience from then on.

I returned to New York, and, soon after, Alec checked into his "home" of forty years, the Algonquin Hotel, and called to tell me he had another piece for me. It was a slow ballad, and he called it "Why?" Different in tempo and feeling from the first one, it nevertheless had the Wilder stamp of bittersweet harmony, and the bass line ascended in half-steps. Alec loves bass lines—"I'd sacrifice melody, *anything* for a good bass line," he says—and many of his songs, notably "It's So Peaceful in the Country," show this obsession with a constantly moving line. His idol is Bach, a clue to his devotion to uninterrupted momentum in the left hand.

New tunes kept coming thick and fast. I couldn't keep up. There are still some I haven't memorized. Alec's output of music of all kinds is prodigious. Having seen the speed and complete concentration with which he composes, I can understand how he gets so much work done, including the great number of classical works he has written—woodwind and brass quintets; pieces for French horn, tuba, flute, wind ensembles, piano; suites and sonatas. The list is endless, the combinations are varied. I have a record by bassist Gary Kerr and Bernie Leighton—"Suite for Bass and Piano." The second movement in this suite is so hauntingly beautiful that I tried to persuade Alec to make a pop song out of it—put lyrics to it. "Oh, no, I can't tamper with it—it's all done. I can't go back to things once they're finished," he says tersely.

He continually writes new pieces and never looks at them again. He hates to hear people talk about the Octets. "Doesn't anybody know I've written *thousands* of pieces since then?" he asks impatiently. He's eager to hear his lesser-known works performed, for though he listens courteously when I play "While We're Young," I know that he'd rather I played something like "The Wrong Blues." But satisfying Alec and pleasing a nightclub audience at the same time isn't always possible.

When I was playing at The Cookery, he was there nightly to listen and give me moral support, and, occasionally, criticism. He is fascinated by improvisation, yet sometimes when someone takes harmonic and melodic liberties with his songs he gets irritated. I've had to listen to many a tirade about this, and many times I've argued with him: "If you want a sheet music performance, it won't be jazz playing." But he insists on his point that at least the first chorus of a tune should be pretty much as the composer wrote it. *"Then* improvise," he says. He was terribly pleased when Paul Desmond said to him not long ago that "the perfect chorus is the song itself."

Incidentally, it isn't only his own songs that Alec worries about. He is as much a watchdog about the songs of other composers. And he is as deeply concerned with the correctness of lyrics as with the notes of a song. He has written the lyrics of some of his own songs ("I'll Be Around," for example) and for the melodies of others ("Where Is the One," with music by Edwin Finckel, beautifully sung by Frank Sinatra). His best-known collaborator has been William Engvick, who wrote the words to "While We're Young," "Who Can I Turn To?" "The April Age," "The Lady Sings the Blues," and, more recently, "I See It Now" and the deeply moving waltz "Remember, My Child." Alec has said that a song needs to be sung to make it truly come alive, and Bill's lyrics prove the point. They remain fresh and evocative, marvels of taste and care for language.

In the years since I first met him, I've seen remarkable new developments taking place in Alec's life and his work. Perhaps the most important and far-reaching event was the launching of his book, *American Popular Song,* in 1972. Edited and with an introduction by writer James T. Maher, this is a unique and valuable work; and even if Alec had never composed a popular song, he could be very proud of the book (which, incidentally, is already considered a "classic"). *American Popular Song* is a searching, detailed, knowledgeable, and often critically humorous analysis of songs by the great composers—Kern, Berlin, Arlen, Rodgers, and so on—and it is a godsend to students of popular music and laymen alike, as well as a joy to musicians, who can refresh their memories when searching for fresh songs to play by a quick glance through its pages. (Typically, Alec has not mentioned any of his own songs in the book.) While not always agreeing with his opinions, one has to respect his convictions and his unequivocal directness in stating his likes and dislikes. For a man who insists he is timid and insecure, Alec comes on strong, with authority and style.

Emotionally, he is very complex. He makes wild swings from an almost childlike gaiety to deep depression. The word *curmudgeon* might have been invented for him. When he is in one of these low moods, it is as if a mistral were blowing. Raging, swirling clouds of pessimistic observations are uttered in a doomsday voice. He speaks morosely of the "great toboggan slide" of "our darkened world." One tries to be cheerful, all to no avail. The only thing to do is to wait till the storm blows over.

Somehow through all these changes of mood, which Alec seems hell-bent on sharing with his friends, the friends all hang on, ready to sweat out the line squalls, wade through the slough of despond, and prepare to revel with him and share the gales of laughter and witty remarks that usually follow one of these gloomy spells. His old friend George Simon, after waiting out one of these moods, once remarked, "I nominate his personality as the one most likely to split."

In 1974 he was the subject of a fascinating profile by Whitney Balliett in *The New Yorker,* which brought him as a person into focus in a very special way. Whitney describes him in his own unique fashion.

"Wilder is a tall man with a big head and small feet. He was wearing a sports jacket, gray slacks, and loafers, and they had a resigned look of strictly functional clothes. He has a long, handsome face and receding gray hair that flows out from the back of his head, giving the impression that he is in constant swift motion. His eyebrows are heavy and curved, and when he has finished making his point—often punctuated by his slamming his fist down on the nearest piece of furniture—they shoot up and the corners of his mouth shoot down. He has piercing, deep-set eyes cushioned by dark, doomsday pouches—diamonds resting on velvet. His face is heavily wrinkled—not with the soft, oh-I-am-growing-old lines but with strong, heavy-weather ones. He has a loud baritone voice and he talks rapidly. When he is agitated, his words roll like cannonballs around the room. He laughs a lot and he swears a lot, in an old-fashioned, Mark Twain manner, and when he is seated he leans forward, like a figurehead breasting a flood tide. A small, serene mustache marks the eye of the hurricane."

Alec's conversation, his comments on people and events, are spoken with a larger-than-life intensity in a resonant baritone that cuts through crowd noise in any room. He could be arrested for noise pollution in the restaurants he patronizes. He could have had a great career in radio. In fact, radio shows he and I have done on WBAI in New York and TV shows in Rochester on Channel 21 have always been highlighted by the clear, strong quality of Alec's voice, his quick wit, great gusts of laughter punctuating eloquently phrased anecdotes and stories, his way of verbally underscoring points with his magic marker voice.

He constantly grumbles about being "forced" into the limelight by being on a television or radio show, yet he comes across on both media with great charm, a strong personality with vitality and humor. One has to know him to understand why he gives himself such a hard time about these things. In actual fact, he is a closet ham—but once he's out onstage, he's *really* on.

To illustrate the point, two years ago he wrote me a piece to perform with the Duke University Wind Ensemble, "Fantasy for Piano and Wind Ensemble." He came along, since he wanted to hear the orchestra play the piece. "Now don't you get me up there to talk during your workshop," he warned me darkly. While I demonstrated a few ideas at the piano for students onstage, he sat in the empty hall, watching. As soon as I suggested he come up and join me in talking to the students, he did so with alacrity, and pretty soon had taken over the workshop, talking, gesturing, making jokes, explaining the music, making the students laugh with his anecdotes, even playing the piano.

Wilder is vocal on many subjects besides music. He rails against long hair and shoulder bags for men and dislikes women wearing pants. "No woman should wear trousers whose crotch doesn't form a V," he insists, giving piercing looks to every pretty girl he sees, raking them from head to toe.

His views are singular, to put it mildly:

> It is inevitable that any of my opinions, especially the negative ones, will be viewed with a degree of condescension due to my age.
>
> Unless a man carries a feedbag reticule slung over his shoulder, wears his hair like Samson, sports railroad engineer jackets, and considers anarchy freedom, his opinions are viewed with bored contempt.
>
> Of course, if he has been stamped with the Good Housekeeping Seal along the way, the New Society is slightly more afraid to dismiss his attitudes.
>
> My life's work is accepted in large measure only by the old and the young. The middle-aged self-proclaimed musical elite dismiss it as traditional, and therefore suspect.
>
> I am interested in only those manifestations of art which, in my estimation, emerge from a profound need to create and an absolute insistence upon a professional point of view. And since I believe that we are living in the heyday of the amateur, I am less inclined to laud their fumbling experimentation than I would if I were convinced that such footling efforts stemmed from deep-rooted conviction and creative compulsion.
>
> The areas in which my weary eyes once again begin to brighten are the music centers; the schools and colleges where the young are overwhelmed by the miracle of music, the discipline of study, the revelations resulting from learning the ethos of interdependence and the infinite rewards implicit in a sane and selfless submission to the demands of musical performance, interpretation and comprehension.
>
> Those who turn to music in order to make money and achieve

notoriety are as contemptible as old ladies' purse snatchers and about as much a part of creation.

The supermarket Wagners who hornswoggle the public into accepting their mongoloid "creations" are as grotesque as the illiterate "philosophers" and "sociological prophets" who whine in assonant rhymes and rummage sale melodies of the sins of the establishment.

The vibrato-less, beady-eyed pseudo-folk singers who, with wretchedly acted-out false modesty, sing of the wind and the rain, the caterpillar and the butterfly, are as specious as the bespangled latter-day troubadors' searching for a God who wears whiskers only at Christmas in front of department stores.

However, I admire those professional musicians who give much of their time and energy to opening the ears of the young to the miracles of honest, forthright jazz, and I admire all those who refuse to be traduced and warped by fashion, by license, and by the clod-stepping march of the barbarians.

To me he is not always just in his criticism of rock, bizarre costumes, long hair—for he, too, is a nonconformist. His insistence on certain clothes, almost a uniform—a worn tweed jacket, gray slacks, and loafers—his refusal to ever wear a tuxedo are the gestures of a rebel.

He reminds me of my father in his Puritan beliefs and intolerance of youthful excesses, and I once told him so.

"I would have liked your father," he replied, smiling.

Obviously Alec is a unique person. A combination of puritanical, old-fashioned ways, yet he can be raunchy, hip, funny. He is aware of everything—new tunes, new books, new sayings, and, above all, the latest gossip. He always carries books. They are his protection and his solace. He can sit on a chair in a hotel lobby and literally disappear into a book.

While sitting in a club listening to music he will sometimes pull out a pad of paper and write letters, or material for one of his many projects. I think that much of the writing for his book *Letters I Never Mailed* was done at a back table in The Cookery while I was working there. He sat night after night, puffing on his pipe, scribbling sheet after sheet from airmail letter pads, stopping only to applaud loudly at the end of each number. Once at the Carlyle when I was playing for a particularly noisy crowd, Alec was at a table behind me, scribbling away. I said waspishly over the mike, "I don't know which is worse, people talking or a guy writing letters while I'm playing." Alec leaned forward and said in a stage whisper, "Yes, but you can't *hear* me."

Howie Richmond, head of the Richmond Organization, recently published most of Alec's popular songs in two beautifully packaged books containing songs that many singers of today would enjoy if they only knew them. I hope some of the young jazz players, with their thirst for interesting tunes with challenging chords to improvise on, will pick up on Alec's pieces. They turn to the newest Chick Corea and Keith Jarrett compositions. But there is room in their repertoires for some Wilder music.

Interestingly, one of the Octets (which were written almost forty years ago) is called "Mama Never Dug That Scene," and in its opening line is very like a piece by Chick Corea—"Matrix." Alec didn't believe me until I played "Matrix" for him. Then he was amazed and I think secretly delighted that he had the idea first. Anybody who thinks his music is old-fashioned should compare these two pieces.

If the young players have not yet caught on to his music, Alec has tuned in to theirs. He likes John Coltrane's "Giant Steps," Chick Corea's "Windows," Bill Evans's "Blue in Green," Stevie Wonder's "All in Love Is Fair," and others.

He spends a lot of his time in nightclubs, listening to jazz. He goes to hear Ellis Larkins, Jimmy Rowles, John Bunch, Tommy Flanagan, Ruby Braff, and many more. He loves Jackie Cain and Roy Kral, Jim Hall, and Stan Getz. He wrote two beautiful pieces for Stan to play with the Boston Pops Orchestra a few years ago.

A musician he reveres is Paul Desmond. He especially likes Paul's jazz chamber music style—appreciating as he does the small groups that favor intricate contrapuntal ideas.

Once we went to The Vanguard to hear Thad Jones and Mel Lewis. He was so attracted to Thad's tune "A Child Is Born" that he went right back to The Algonquin and wrote a lyric for it, which is one of the finest things he's ever done, a masterpiece of simplicity.

Alec often talks about his unhappy childhood. He remembers being lonely and withdrawn as a youngster. But he has used all the different sides to his nature in his music. The humor, the lively sense of fun, his warmth and generosity show in the richness and color of his orchestral writing. Romanticism flows through the melodic lines and is woven into the intricate contrapuntal patterns that are so much a part of his writing. And through it all lingers a bittersweet, wistful quality, an unfulfilled longing, like a whisper from bygone days. Some of his songs evoke romantic mind-pictures: a girl in a crinoline dancing on a sunlit lawn, trees heavy with silence on a windless night, the moon reflected in a dew-pond shining in the high grass. The fact that his writing has this pastoral quality, like English folk music, is not surprising. Delius was among Alec's many influences. He is also passionately fond of the countryside and the peace of sleepy villages.

His range and scope is so broad that it can change from a simple melodic phrase to complex voicings, all in the same tune. He is a master when it comes to combining inner voices so that each will stand on its own as a separate melody, weaving cobweb patterns that stretch out in all directions, their lines crossing yet always logical and musical, always in harmony.

Alec's large output of classical music will soon be made more accessible by Gunther Schuller, who is collecting and collating it; Gunther's own company, Margun, will soon publish it. So much of Alec's music has been unavailable because of the way he writes pieces and just tosses them aside. Now, through the painstaking work of tuba virtuoso Harvey Phillips, who has collected Alec's music for years and has now passed the manuscripts on to Gunther, much of this vast body of sonatas, suites, and other works will for the first time be available to everybody.

Alec seems very cheered by this. There seems to be an increasing desire on his part to have his music played and to work at getting it organized and available. And now his radio and TV appearances are multiplying, and he seems much more willing to get involved in these and other new projects. The series of programs on *American Popular Song* he is taping on Public Broadcast Radio, featuring singers Teddi King, Barbara Lea, Jackie Cain, Mabel Mercer, David Allen, Johnny Hartman, and others, will be heard throughout the country this fall. Some of the singers will be doing Alec Wilder songs (including some new ones)—and all because they wanted to.

Alec has written songs that have lasted, full of daring and musical strength. Their uniqueness lies in their structure, their craftsmanship. Their distinguishing mark, always fresh, is their care and good taste.

To me, his music transcends all fashions and fads. He has the courage and experience to write what *he* wants regardless of how it relates to today's market. And that, I believe, is our good fortune, for there is so much for musicians to discover in his music. He is not the type to compose contrived songs for the Top 40. Any talk of such matters sends him off on a tirade against commercialism. Naturally, this way of thinking has made public acceptance hard for him to attain, because he is always swimming against the great popular tide.

But this is his way, and he writes as if his life depends on it. Maybe it does.

1976

POSTSCRIPT

Alec Wilder died in Gainesville, Florida, on Christmas Eve 1980, from a recurrence of the cancer that he suffered in 1975. It's ironic that he died on Christmas Eve. It was a day he was not fond of; in fact, he disliked all holidays, perhaps because he had no family, and one could sense that he was especially lonely at these times. He railed away at the commercialization of the holidays; he never gave Christmas presents or sent cards (or gave any sign that he had received any). Instead, he would disappear to some remote place. One Christmas Day he called from the Jared Coffin House in Nantucket, elated at having found the place deserted. He talked of walking by the ocean in the crisp, cold air, with the winter sun shining on the water. It all seemed just the right thing for him to be doing at that time.

I miss Alec. I miss his outrageous sense of humor, his tirades against bad music and fast food, his knowledge of nature and compassion for all wild creatures, the books he read and then gave to his friends. He had many gifts to give, and he was generous with all of them—his time, his support and encouragement. But his greatest gift and the most lasting one of all was his music.

Alec always said his music would become more popular after his death. He used to grumble about having written pieces that he said had never been played. He mentioned a certain ballad that he had written and, banging his fist on the table, which he often did when he was annoyed, yelled, "I've never heard it performed. NOT EVEN ONCE!"

In almost every year since his death, an Alec Wilder tribute concert has taken place close to Alec's birthday, February 16, and many of his friends, such as Jackie Cain and Roy Kral, Marlene Verplanck, Barbara Lea, and I have performed. Originally organized by the virtuoso tuba player Harvey Phillips, the concerts are getting harder to arrange now that Harvey has retired. However, Susannah McCorkle recently performed a program of Alec's music on my radio show *Piano Jazz,* and Alec Wilder fans contacted us in droves by e-mail, fax, and letters to say how much they enjoyed it.

There have been many more performances of Alec's compositions by jazz musicians such as pianists Roland Hanna and Keith Jarrett, and I myself put out a CD of some of my favorite Wilder tunes. His classical pieces are played a great deal by college orchestras, and I look forward to the day when some of his many interesting (and sometimes quirky) orchestral works will be performed at Carnegie Hall.

Last year photographer Louis Ouzer, his wife, Helen, and I made a trip to Avon, New York, to visit Alec's grave. The locust tree that I had arranged to have planted there looked beautiful, and Louis, full of fun as usual, pulled out a pipe and a can of soap suds and started blowing bubbles. This was something that Alec had loved to do. In many ways he was like a little kid. I recall that on one of my visits to Rochester we were hanging out at Louis's studio. That day Alec felt like blowing bubbles, and the two of us were standing in the street, having a really good time, when a pompous little man from the Eastman School walked by. Looking at us with great disapproval, he said, "Alec Wilder, you'll *never* grow up!" As he went by Alec hollered, "No, I never will," and the two of us stood there, laughing our heads off. A few minutes later Louis came out of the studio and took a photograph of us, which shows Alec in one of his happiest moments. This photo has been circulated everywhere, in books and magazines, and it always reminds me of Alec's funeral, which was attended by many of his good friends. Singing duo Jackie and Roy were among them, and sad though the occasion was, we were heartened by a beautiful trumpet solo, Alec's tender ballad "It's So Peaceful in the Country" played by Sal Sparazza. As the sounds carried on the light wind that fluttered the leaves on the big trees surrounding us, the irrepressible Louis took out his bubble pipe and soap suds and handed pipes to all of us. We then blew some gorgeous bubbles over the grave. Alec would have loved it, and I like to think that somewhere among the trees, with the sun shining down on us all, Alec was listening and enjoying it. It was a very special moment.

Marian McPartland is widely acknowledged as one of the world's most skilled practitioners of jazz piano. She has been a force on the jazz scene since the 1950s and has recorded more than sixty albums and CDs. In addition to her touring schedule, she has hosted *Marian McPartland's Piano Jazz* since its inception in 1978. The series is the longest-running cultural program on National Public Radio. It won the coveted Peabody Award in 1984, the ASCAP–Deems Taylor Award in 1991, the New York Festival's Gold World Medal (1998), and the 2001 Gracie Allen Award presented by the Foundation of American Women in Radio and Television.

Among other honors, McPartland was named one of the American Jazz Masters for the year 2000 by the National Endowment for the Arts, received a Lifetime Achievement Award from *Down Beat* magazine, and was honored by the Kennedy Center with the Mary Lou Williams Women in Jazz Award.

McPartland continues to keep up a pace and range of activities that would exhaust most people half her age, recording regularly for Concord Jazz, taping new segments of *Piano Jazz,* and performing around the world. She shows no signs of slowing down, which is good news for jazz.

James T. Maher writes about, and is a noted historian of, jazz, musical theater, and popular music. He edited and wrote the introduction for Alec Wilder's *American Popular Song: The Great Innovators, 1900–1950.*

Music in American Life

Heartland Excursions: Ethnomusicological Reflections on Schools of
Music   *Bruno Nettl*
Doowop: The Chicago Scene   *Robert Pruter*
Blue Rhythms: Six Lives in Rhythm and Blues   *Chip Deffaa*
Shoshone Ghost Dance Religion: Poetry Songs and Great Basin
Context   *Judith Vander*
Go Cat Go! Rockabilly Music and Its Makers   *Craig Morrison*
'Twas Only an Irishman's Dream: The Image of Ireland and the Irish in
American Popular Song Lyrics, 1800–1920   *William H. A. Williams*
Democracy at the Opera: Music, Theater, and Culture in New York City,
1815–60   *Karen Ahlquist*
Fred Waring and the Pennsylvanians   *Virginia Waring*
Woody, Cisco, and Me: Seamen Three in the Merchant Marine
Jim Longhi
Behind the Burnt Cork Mask: Early Blackface Minstrelsy and Antebellum
American Popular Culture   *William J. Mahar*
Going to Cincinnati: A History of the Blues in the Queen City
Steven C. Tracy
Pistol Packin' Mama: Aunt Molly Jackson and the Politics of
Folksong   *Shelly Romalis*
Sixties Rock: Garage, Psychedelic, and Other Satisfactions   *Michael Hicks*
The Late Great Johnny Ace and the Transition from R&B to Rock 'n'
Roll   *James M. Salem*
Tito Puente and the Making of Latin Music   *Steven Loza*
Juilliard: A History   *Andrea Olmstead*
Understanding Charles Seeger, Pioneer in American Musicology
Edited by Bell Yung and Helen Rees
Mountains of Music: West Virginia Traditional Music from
Goldenseal   Edited by John Lilly
Alice Tully: An Intimate Portrait   *Albert Fuller*
A Blues Life   *Henry Townsend, as told to Bill Greensmith*
Long Steel Rail: The Railroad in American Folksong (2d ed.)   *Norm Cohen*
The Golden Age of Gospel   *Text by Horace Clarence Boyer; photography by
Lloyd Yearwood*
Aaron Copland: The Life and Work of an Uncommon Man
Howard Pollack
Louis Moreau Gottschalk   *S. Frederick Starr*
Race, Rock, and Elvis   *Michael T. Bertrand*

The University of Illinois Press
is a founding member of the
Association of American University Presses.

Composed in 9/14 ITC Stone Serif
with Helvetica Neue display
by Celia Shapland
for the University of Illinois Press
Designed by Paula Newcomb
Manufactured by Thomson-Shore, Inc.

University of Illinois Press
1325 South Oak Street
Champaign, IL 61820-6903
www.press.uillinois.edu